# Seaplanes at War

## A Treasury of Words and Pictures

### First Edition

## DONALD H. SWEET

Copies of this book may be purchased by sending a check for
$27.00 plus $5.00 s/h, for each copy ordered, to:
Mr. D.W. Sweet
135 Woodland Avenue
Ridgewood, NJ 07450

Front cover photo: A rare sight: PBMs in formation, heading west over the Pacific. (L. H. Roberts photo collection)

ISBN-0-923687-51-3
Library of Congress Catalog Card Number 98-83263

Copyright © 1999 by Donald H. Sweet
All rights reserved.
Printed in the United States of America

No part of this book may be reproduced or transmitted in any form or by any means, electronic or mechanical, including photocopying, recording, or by any information storage and retrieval system, without the written permission of the publisher, except where permitted by law.

# DEDICATION

We will always remember with deep affection those shipmates who flew out but did not return; those who did not grow old as the rest of us have. It was our great privilege to have known them. They live on in our memories. We shall never forget them, and I dedicate this book to them. They made the sacrifices that make this story real.

Frank Hanning, a veteran of VPB-28—Mariner Patrol Bombing Squadron 28—has been most helpful to me as I wrote this story. He has provided information that I would not otherwise have found. One of the really interesting things was an incomplete poem by a petty officer in VPB-28 named Charles Boyle, a bow turret gunner. Before he had a chance to finish his poem, he was killed in action over the South China Sea flying a Black Cat mission. It is printed here:

> But in this victorious moment . . . what of the deceased?
> The bloody days of war have ceased.
> Lights are glittering, bells are ringing,
> Whistles are blowing, crowds are singing;
>
> Our loved ones now only a memory.
> Some blond and tall; others dark and small,
> Brave, sturdy men—they answered the call
>
> To destiny—the malicious enemy.
> To our fallen comrades over there
> In jungles, on the beaches, in quiet lanes,
> On burning ships, in flaming planes,
>
> Our Father, to you they have come,
> Victims of the stormy nights
> Martyrs of Thee for the Holy Rights,
>
> Our gold stars lead them home.
> Father, hear our humble voices,
> Hear our sincere wishes,
> Gather them that we miss.
> For them we offer this prayer.
>
> —Charles Boyle
> *Killed in action, March 8, 1945, on a mission over the South China Sea*

# CONTENTS

List of Illustrations . . . . . . . . . . . . . . . . . . . . . . . . . . . . . . . . . xi
Foreword by Nevins Frankel (Mr. Patrol Squadron) . . . . . . . . . . . xix
Preface . . . . . . . . . . . . . . . . . . . . . . . . . . . . . . . . . . . . . . . . . xxi
A Letter to My Readers . . . . . . . . . . . . . . . . . . . . . . . . . . . . xxiii
Map . . . . . . . . . . . . . . . . . . . . . . . . . . . . . . . . . . . . . . . . . . xxiv

THE ISLANDS . . . . . . . . . . . . . . . . . . . . . . . . . . . . . . . . . . . 1
    Overview . . . . . . . . . . . . . . . . . . . . . . . . . . . . . . . . . . . . 3
    Moving on . . . . . . . . . . . . . . . . . . . . . . . . . . . . . . . . . . . 8
    The Southwest Pacific . . . . . . . . . . . . . . . . . . . . . . . . . . . 9
    Back to the Philippines . . . . . . . . . . . . . . . . . . . . . . . . . . 10
    The Central Pacific . . . . . . . . . . . . . . . . . . . . . . . . . . . . . 11

THE PLANES . . . . . . . . . . . . . . . . . . . . . . . . . . . . . . . . . . . 21
    Overview . . . . . . . . . . . . . . . . . . . . . . . . . . . . . . . . . . . 22
    The Politics of War . . . . . . . . . . . . . . . . . . . . . . . . . . . . 22
    The PBM Comes of Age . . . . . . . . . . . . . . . . . . . . . . . . . 24
    The Martin Mariner . . . . . . . . . . . . . . . . . . . . . . . . . . . . 25
    The Marianas and Palaus . . . . . . . . . . . . . . . . . . . . . . . . . 27
    JATO . . . . . . . . . . . . . . . . . . . . . . . . . . . . . . . . . . . . . . 31
    Big Bird . . . . . . . . . . . . . . . . . . . . . . . . . . . . . . . . . . . . 31
    It's a Long Runway . . . . . . . . . . . . . . . . . . . . . . . . . . . . 31
    The Art of Buoy Making . . . . . . . . . . . . . . . . . . . . . . . . . 32
    Alone and Dangerous . . . . . . . . . . . . . . . . . . . . . . . . . . . 33
    Our Worst Enemy . . . . . . . . . . . . . . . . . . . . . . . . . . . . . 34
    Buoy Watch: A Way of Life . . . . . . . . . . . . . . . . . . . . . . 34
    The Irreplaceable PATSUs . . . . . . . . . . . . . . . . . . . . . . . . 36
    The "Good News, Bad News" Mariner . . . . . . . . . . . . . . . 36
    A Little Humor Goes a Long Way . . . . . . . . . . . . . . . . . . 38

# THE MEN AND THEIR SQUADRONS . . . . . . . . . . . . . 53
## THE MEN . . . . . . . . . . . . . . . . . . . . . . . . . 54
### Overview . . . . . . . . . . . . . . . . . . . . . . . . 54
### Heroes . . . . . . . . . . . . . . . . . . . . . . . . . 54
### Camaraderie . . . . . . . . . . . . . . . . . . . . . . 57
### Something Special . . . . . . . . . . . . . . . . . . . 58
### The Glue That Held It All Together . . . . . . . . . . 60
### The Men Speak . . . . . . . . . . . . . . . . . . . . . 61
### A Fitting Epilogue . . . . . . . . . . . . . . . . . . 62

## THE SQUADRONS . . . . . . . . . . . . . . . . . . . . . 63
### VH and VPB Squadron Overview . . . . . . . . . . . . . 63
### The Pioneers . . . . . . . . . . . . . . . . . . . . . 65
### Patrol Bombing Squadron 16 (VPB-16) . . . . . . . . . 66
### Patrol Bombing Squadron 17 (VPB-17) . . . . . . . . . 67
### Patrol Bombing Squadron 18 (VPB-18) . . . . . . . . . 69
### Patrol Bombing Squadron 19 (VPB-19) . . . . . . . . . 72
### Patrol Bombing Squadron 20 (VPB-20) . . . . . . . . . 74
### Patrol Bombing Squadron 21 (VPB-21) . . . . . . . . . 78
### Patrol Bombing Squadron 22 (VPB-22) . . . . . . . . . 81
### Patrol Bombing Squadron 25 (VPB-25) . . . . . . . . . 87
### Patrol Bombing Squadron 26 (VPB-26) . . . . . . . . . 88
### Patrol Bombing Squadron 27 (VPB-27) . . . . . . . . . 89
### Patrol Bombing Squadron 28 (VPB-28) . . . . . . . . . 91
### Patrol Bombing Squadron 202 (VPB-202) . . . . . . . . 92
### Patrol Bombing Squadron 205 (VPB-205) . . . . . . . . 94
### Patrol Bombing Squadron 208 (VPB-208) . . . . . . . . 95
### Patrol Bombing Squadron 216 (VPB-216) . . . . . . . . 97
### VH Squadrons Get Their Man . . . . . . . . . . . . . . 99
### The Almost Forgotten Heroes . . . . . . . . . . . . . 101
### Rescue Squadron VH-3 . . . . . . . . . . . . . . . . . 101
### Rescue Squadron VH-1 . . . . . . . . . . . . . . . . . 102
### VH Squadrons Never Fail . . . . . . . . . . . . . . . 102
### VH Squadron History . . . . . . . . . . . . . . . . . 103

*Plane P-1 of VPB-202, the first PBM squadron sent to the Pacific. They were the pioneers we all followed and learned from. The officers are, left to right, Kagle, Kreitzer, Leeman, and Caffarel. Leeman piloted P-1. (William Kreitzer photo collection)*

| | |
|---|---|
| **THE SHIPS** | 127 |
|     Changing Roles | 128 |
|     Classes of Tenders | 129 |
|     Jonah in the Whale | 133 |
|     The PATSUs | 133 |
|     The AVPs | 134 |
| | |
| **THE WAR ENDS** | 139 |
|     Overview | 141 |
|     Surprise, Surprise | 141 |
|     Suicide as a Weapon | 142 |
|     The Bomb | 149 |
|     Democracy Awakes | 149 |
|     Apology? | 150 |
|     The Last Word | 150 |
| | |
| A Tough and Homely Old Bird | 151 |
| Come Fly with Me | 153 |
| Epilogue | 155 |
| Key Contributors | 157 |
| Glossary | 163 |
| Sources Cited | 171 |
| About the Author | 173 |

# ILLUSTRATIONS

Plane P-1 of VPB-202 . . . . . . . . . . . . . . . . . . . . . . . . . . . . . . . x
The Marines have landed on Saipan . . . . . . . . . . . . . . . . . . . . . . . xi

## THE ISLANDS

Parry Island shortly after naval bombardment in 1944 . . . . . . . . . . . . . 1
Kerama-retto gardens—a good place to catch a snake! . . . . . . . . . . . 2
Babelthuap Island, in the Palaus . . . . . . . . . . . . . . . . . . . . . . . . 2
Two more that will never fly again for Hirohito . . . . . . . . . . . . . . . 3
The original john on Parry Island—a fly's paradise! . . . . . . . . . . . . 4
Our modern tent city on Parry Island, 1945 . . . . . . . . . . . . . . . . . . 4
Parry Island "sanitation department" sign . . . . . . . . . . . . . . . . . . 5
Three VPB-25 guys looking over a downed Japanese float plane . . . . . . 6
Suicide cliff on Saipan . . . . . . . . . . . . . . . . . . . . . . . . . . . . . . 7
The ramp and a burned-out Japanese hangar at Tanapag seaplane base . . . 8
Iwo Jima's anchorage . . . . . . . . . . . . . . . . . . . . . . . . . . . . . . 9
Kerama-retto on a quiet afternoon . . . . . . . . . . . . . . . . . . . . . . 10
Kerama-retto with the AVP USS *Mackinac* . . . . . . . . . . . . . . . . . 11
Iwo Jima's D-day (February 1945) . . . . . . . . . . . . . . . . . . . . . . . 12
Three armed guards from VPB-205 on Saipan, April 1945 . . . . . . . . . 13
Wake Island just prior to final surrender in 1945 . . . . . . . . . . . . . . 13
Waikiki Beach in front of the Royal Hawaiian Hotel . . . . . . . . . . . . 14
MGM's western Pacific franchise—Parry Island, Eniwetok . . . . . . . . . 14
VPB-216's housecleaning day at Parry Island . . . . . . . . . . . . . . . . 15
Up, up, and away from Tanapag to Yap today . . . . . . . . . . . . . . . . 15
Los Negros in the Admiralties . . . . . . . . . . . . . . . . . . . . . . . . . 16
The ramp at Hilo, Hawaii . . . . . . . . . . . . . . . . . . . . . . . . . . . . 16
A "gift" from OOD at Kaneohe, Hawaii . . . . . . . . . . . . . . . . . . . 17
VPB-21's ground crew . . . . . . . . . . . . . . . . . . . . . . . . . . . . . . 17

"Washing machine" on Saipan . . . . . . . . . . . . . . . . . . . . . . . . . . 18
"Washing machine" on Parry Island, Eniwetok . . . . . . . . . . . . . . . . 18
Laundry and housekeeping day at Saipan . . . . . . . . . . . . . . . . . . 19
"Suicide Gap" at Kerama-retto, with kamikazes on the attack . . . . . . . . 20

## THE PLANES

One of VPB-21's PBM-3Ds taking off from Eniwetok . . . . . . . . . . . . 21
"Up, up and away. We are off to visit Iwo again today." . . . . . . . . . . 22
A PBM-5 on patrol just east of the Japanese coast . . . . . . . . . . . . . 24
A PBM-5's cockpit . . . . . . . . . . . . . . . . . . . . . . . . . . . . . . . 25
The navigator's and flight engineer's stations of a PBM-5 . . . . . . . . . 25
A cutaway picture of the PBM-5 . . . . . . . . . . . . . . . . . . . . . . . 26
A PBM-5's galley . . . . . . . . . . . . . . . . . . . . . . . . . . . . . . . . 27
Consolidated's PB2Y Coronado . . . . . . . . . . . . . . . . . . . . . . . . 28
A Black Cat PBM of VPB-28 . . . . . . . . . . . . . . . . . . . . . . . . . 29
A PBY-5A Catalina from VPB-54 . . . . . . . . . . . . . . . . . . . . . . 29
A PBM-5 with its JATO mechanism mounted on its wings . . . . . . . . 30
A JATO takeoff at Kerama-retto . . . . . . . . . . . . . . . . . . . . . . . 30
A sailor aviator with expended JATO bottles after takeoff . . . . . . . . . 31
A VPB-19 JATO takeoff from Iwo Jima . . . . . . . . . . . . . . . . . . . 31
Singling up at buoy . . . . . . . . . . . . . . . . . . . . . . . . . . . . . . 33
Two photos of relief crews arriving at a plane at buoy . . . . . . . . . . . 35
Ever-constant engine maintenance, on Eniwetok . . . . . . . . . . . . . . 36
VPB-21, crew 14, discussing an engine problem aboard the *Chandeleur* . . . . 37
Ain't JATO wonderful? . . . . . . . . . . . . . . . . . . . . . . . . . . . . 38
Two PBM-5s that didn't survive a typhoon at Okinawa . . . . . . . . . . 39
Another PBM-5 that didn't survive a typhoon at Okinawa . . . . . . . . 39
A PBM-3 launching from the ramp at NAS Key West, Florida . . . . . . . 40
A bad night landing at Harvey Point, North Carolina . . . . . . . . . . . 41
"Old Reliable"—the PBY Catalina (Black Cat) . . . . . . . . . . . . . . . 42
The ordnance crew loads an aerial torpedo called Fido . . . . . . . . . . 43
Ready for any ship tonight! . . . . . . . . . . . . . . . . . . . . . . . . . 43
Vance Kyle of Box 10, the "Mighty Ten-der" of VPB-17 . . . . . . . . . . 44
The ever-busy ramp at NAS Kaneohe Bay, Hawaii . . . . . . . . . . . . . 44
*Sexy Anna*, all shot up, barely made it back to Kerama-retto . . . . . . . . 45
A VPB-19 Mariner leaves Tanapag seadrome, Saipan, for Iwo Jima . . . . . 46

VPB-13's PB2Y Coronado just back from the China coast . . . . . . . . . . 46
A 40mm shell went through the starboard wings of this Mariner . . . . . . . 47
VPB-21, crew 17, comes aboard the USS *Chandeleur* for some hull repair . . . 47
VPB-216's Mariner fueled up and tied down at buoy at Saipan . . . . . . . 48
VPB-13's PB2Y5 taxis into Kerama-retto . . . . . . . . . . . . . . 48
A Harvey Point, North Carolina, plane on the ramp at NAS Key West, Florida 49
V-2 of VPB-21, at buoy in Kerama-retto on a rare calm day . . . . . . . . 49
A PBM-3D coming aboard its tender by crane, for repair . . . . . . . . . 50
The PBM-3 is secured diagonally to conserve deck space on the tender . . . . 51
VPB-16's plane No. 11 crosses paths with VPB-21's V6 . . . . . . . . . . 52

## THE MEN AND THEIR SQUADRONS

Purple Heart award ceremony, USS *Chandeleur* . . . . . . . . . . . . . 53
Several of the stalwarts with a local Filipino young lady . . . . . . . . . 54
The O Club at Tanapag, Saipan . . . . . . . . . . . . . . . . . . 54
Four of "Norm's bad boys" on liberty in Honolulu, July 1944 . . . . . . . . 55
Two of the guys with a local buddy in the Philippines . . . . . . . . . . 56
Five of VPB-216 enjoying the sights and sounds of San Diego . . . . . . . 56
Crew 6, VPB-28, preparing for a Black Cat night; Jinamoc Island . . . . . . 57
VPB-20 crew ready for a Black Cat night out of Leyte Gulf . . . . . . . . 58
VPB-216's Olympic ski team, 1944 . . . . . . . . . . . . . . . . . 58
VPB-205 before heading west from Kaneohe Bay, Hawaii . . . . . . . . . 58
VPB-28 after a difficult night at the CPO Club . . . . . . . . . . . . 59
A group of VPB-21ers the last night before leaving for Okinawa . . . . . . 59
Hula dancers and cold beer on the way to the war . . . . . . . . . . . 60
VPB-21 crewmen on Saipan . . . . . . . . . . . . . . . . . . . 60
Some of the overflow from the O Club on Mogmog . . . . . . . . . . . 61
Five of VPB-21's crew enjoying a few "premium" beers on Mogmog . . . . . 61
Simms and Moriarty of VPB-21 . . . . . . . . . . . . . . . . . . 62
A group of "old salts" from VPB-21 . . . . . . . . . . . . . . . . 62
Two Mariners on the field at Harvey Point, North Carolina . . . . . . . . 63
Gassing up on the ramp at Harvey Point, North Carolina . . . . . . . . . 64
P-9 of VPB-202 resting at buoy in Tanapag, Saipan . . . . . . . . . . . 64
A VPB-20 PBM-3D cruising the Pacific . . . . . . . . . . . . . . . 65
Box 10, the "Mighty Ten-der" of VPB-17, on the way to Saipan . . . . . . 67
A bunch of the big birds on the water at Kerama-retto . . . . . . . . . . 68

| | |
|---|---|
| Plane 13 of VPB-17 tied up at buoy, Saipan, October 1944 | 69 |
| A VPB-18 Mariner shot down by a Japanese fighter | 70 |
| Harvey Herzog, VPB-18, playing pilot | 70 |
| Harvey Herzog, VPB-18, pours it on to a Japanese ship, South China Sea | 71 |
| A Japanese ship in the South China Sea being attacked by VPB-18 | 71 |
| VPB-18's tally sheet—about the best in the Pacific Mariner community | 72 |
| The USS *Hamlin* at Iwo Jima | 72 |
| Crew 14 of VPB-19 takes it slow and easy | 73 |
| A well-prepared buoy watch on a VPB-19 Mariner at Iwo Jima | 74 |
| The enlisted contingent of VPB-20 posing in their dress blues | 75 |
| Officers of VPB-20 in their dress blues | 76 |
| A VPB-20 Black Cat being lifted aboard the USS *Tangier* for engine work | 77 |
| A VPB-20 Black Cat coming on board the USS *Tangier* | 77 |
| Original personnel of VPB-21, June 1944, Kaneohe, Hawaii | 78 |
| Crew 14 of VPB-21 posing by *Charlot the Harlot* | 79 |
| The *Yamato* under way on a suicide run to defend Okinawa | 80 |
| The *Yamato* on fire and sinking after being attacked | 80 |
| Dick Simms and John Hook fighting off five Japanese Georges | 81 |
| A Japanese fighter drops a phosphorus bomb near V-10—with no effect | 82 |
| A Japanese fighter makes a pass at Simms's plane (V10) | 82 |
| Simms trying to evade a Japanese fighter—too late | 83 |
| Six of V-10's crew in two life rafts | 84 |
| Four of V-10's men awaiting pickup by a Dumbo plane from VH-3 | 84 |
| Pilot of a PBM that dropped four bombs on the *Yamato*—shot down | 85 |
| Crew of V-8 getting on board VH-3's Mariner after a night afloat | 86 |
| Six guys on the tail—"It's a big plane, isn't it?" | 87 |
| VPB-22, crew 11, 1944–1945 | 87 |
| Ltjg. Croze of VPB-20, made it back to the Celebes | 88 |
| VPB-25, January 1945, Jinamoc Island | 89 |
| VPB-27 takes off from Oahu, Hawaii, after some R&R | 90 |
| VPB-27, crew 2's E2, *Dinah Might* | 90 |
| VPB-27's crew 2 | 91 |
| Five of the stalwarts from VPB-27 | 91 |
| VPB-28's plane 108, a Black Cat, at the buoy at Tawitawi | 92 |
| The VPB-28 ready room on Jinamoc Island | 92 |
| The crash boat that towed D-2, VPB-28, back to Leyte | 93 |

| | |
|---|---|
| D-2, VPB-28, forced down by engine trouble, being towed back to Leyte | 93 |
| VPB-28 skipper and crew after a long day at the office | 94 |
| The USS *Curtiss* at Kerama-retto | 95 |
| VPB-208's D-15 in a losing battle with Kerama-retto's rough waters | 96 |
| Help comes to VPB-208's D-15 in Kerama-retto's rough waters | 97 |
| Two of VPB-208's PBM-3Ds cruising | 98 |
| The best-looking rudder in the Navy—VPB-216's | 99 |
| VPB-216 was known for always finishing any job they started | 99 |
| VPB-216, crew 14, downed near Yap Island, awaiting rescue | 100 |
| Hashmark-9 of VPB-216 at buoy and settled for the night | 100 |
| Lee Roy Way of VH-3 lights one up for a rescued aircrew member | 101 |
| A B-25 bomber crew picked up by one of VH-3's planes | 103 |
| VPB-28's office, meeting room, and duty station on Jinamoc, 1945 | 104 |
| Norm Lorentzsen lectures on moderation in all things | 105 |
| VPB-25 personnel off to morning chow | 105 |
| Norm Lorentzsen on the radar dome of V-1 | 106 |
| Since scotch was a little hard to find at Palau "Coca-Cola was the one" | 106 |
| Loading bombs onto a repaired PBM | 107 |
| VPB-27's E-11 gassing up from an AVP | 107 |
| Tail gunners from VPB-16 | 108 |
| Tail gunners from VPB-216 | 108 |
| Crew 14, VPB-21, drops a bomb directly on a pier and four barges | 109 |
| Cleaning a waist gun at Kerama-retto—a buoy-watch task | 109 |
| Crew 14, VPB-21, sinks a Japanese lugger off the coast of Korea | 110 |
| A Sugar Dog about to be attacked by a VPB-21 Mariner | 110 |
| V-14, VPB-21, attacks a pier, a Sugar Dog, and several luggers | 111 |
| A strafing run on a pier just bombed by V-14 of VPB-21 | 111 |
| A Japanese freighter under attack off the coast of Korea | 112 |
| The above Japanese freighter is left heavily damaged and smoking | 113 |
| A Japanese gunboat under way and under attack from a VPB-208 plane | 114 |
| Crews 14 and 16, VPB-21, attack a small Japanese bulk carrier | 115 |
| The above bulk carrier, just before it sank | 115 |
| Japanese mine layer, forty miles out of Shanghai, about to be attacked | 116 |
| A Sugar Dog off the coast of Korea, about to be attacked by VPB-21 | 117 |
| VPB-21's crew 16 sinks a Sugar Dog, May 1945, in the China Sea | 117 |
| A Japanese Jill fighter downed near Aguni-shima | 118 |

Kusakaki-shima's radio-radar installation is bombed . . . . . . . . . . . . . . . . 118
Attack on a lighthouse and radar station in southern Japan, April 1945 . . . . 119
A Sugar Dog going under in the China Sea, August 1945 . . . . . . . . . . 119
Sugar Dog under way . . . . . . . . . . . . . . . . . . . . . . . . . . . . . . 120
The same Sugar Dog—"Now you see it, now you don't" . . . . . . . . . . 120
Two Sugar Dogs attacked by VPB-21 in the South China Sea . . . . . . . . 121
Three views of a Sugar Dog under fire, May 1945 . . . . . . . . . . 122–123
Crew 7 chases a Sugar Dog and finally get a bomb amidships . . . . . . . 123
A VPB-27 Mariner hit by a 40mm shell—where it went in . . . . . . . . 124
The above shell, where it came out—without exploding . . . . . . . . . . 124
A. D. Brown, VPB-21's crew 6, checking 20mm holes in the rudder . . . . . 125
A VPB-27 E-2 being hurried aboard its tender after battle . . . . . . . . 125
Crew 12, VPB-21, downed between Eniwetok and Wake, in their life rafts . . 126

## THE SHIPS

The USS *Hamlin* . . . . . . . . . . . . . . . . . . . . . . . . . . . . . . . . 127
The USS *Curtiss* . . . . . . . . . . . . . . . . . . . . . . . . . . . . . . . . 128
The USS *Hamlin* under way . . . . . . . . . . . . . . . . . . . . . . . . . 129
An AVP fueling two Mariners at Leyte Bay, Philippines . . . . . . . . . . . 130
The USS *Mackinac* at anchor in Kerama-retto, July 1945 . . . . . . . . . . 130
Dog Victor 4 of VPB-21 ready to get under way at Kerama-retto . . . . . . 131
The USS *Chandeleur*, AV-10, tied up at Saipan, August 1944 . . . . . . . . 131
The USS *Shelikof* . . . . . . . . . . . . . . . . . . . . . . . . . . . . . . . 132
The USS *Shelikof* (AVP) at anchor in Kerama-retto . . . . . . . . . . . . . 132
A U.S. destroyer backs away from the USS *Chandeleur* . . . . . . . . . . . 133
A U.S. submarine off the coast of Formosa, May 1945 . . . . . . . . . . . . 134
A whaleboat heads for its AVP with buoy-watch change . . . . . . . . . . 134
A disabled Japanese freighter in Tanapag Harbor, Saipan . . . . . . . . . . 135
A U.S. destroyer picks up crew 14, VPB-216, near Yap Island, July 1944 . . . . 135
Mail arrives aboard the USS *Chandeleur* . . . . . . . . . . . . . . . . . . 136
A hot game of volleyball on the USS *Tangier* . . . . . . . . . . . . . . . 136
Frances Langford, a movie actress on a USO tour to the Far East . . . . . 137
The *Chandeleur*'s air force on the seaplane deck—"Grumman Duck" . . . . . 137
Broadway comes to the USS *Hamlin*—Christmas 1945 . . . . . . . . . . . 138

## THE WAR ENDS

A section of Nagasaki after the bomb . . . . . . . . . . . . . . . . . 139  
The imperial palace in Tokyo shows no damage from the U.S. bombs . . . . 140  
Debris and emptiness after the U.S. atomic bomb on Nagasaki . . . . . . 141  
Kamikazes attack the USS *Hamlin* . . . . . . . . . . . . . . . . . . 142  
A kamikaze hit on the USS *Hamlin* seaplane deck . . . . . . . . . . . 143  
A section of Nagasaki after the bomb . . . . . . . . . . . . . . . . . 144  
Japanese soldiers captured by a crew from the USS *Chandeleur* and VPB-21. . 144  
Sequence of 6 photos—Japanese envoys changing planes before surrendering:  
The first Betty arrives . . . . . . . . . . . . . . . . . . . . . . . 146  
A Betty taxis past an armed guard . . . . . . . . . . . . . . . . . . 146  
No formal reception here . . . . . . . . . . . . . . . . . . . . . . 147  
A Betty parked with armed guards . . . . . . . . . . . . . . . . . . 147  
A group of Japanese envoys . . . . . . . . . . . . . . . . . . . . . 148  
The envoys board a US plane—for the Philippines and surrender . . . . . 148  
A devastated section of Nagasaki—nothing left . . . . . . . . . . . . 149  

## BACK MATTER

VPB-21 Mariner at buoy off Parry Island, Eniwetok, August 1944 . . . . . 151  
A PBM-5 "on the step" . . . . . . . . . . . . . . . . . . . . . . . . 152  
The usual "smooth water" at Kossol Passage . . . . . . . . . . . . . . 153  
"There are no flowers on a sailor's grave" . . . . . . . . . . . . . . 154  
A B-29 bomber north of Saipan found by crew 2, VPB-27 . . . . . . . . 155  
Vance Kyle, crew 10, VPB-17 . . . . . . . . . . . . . . . . . . . . . 156  
Spud Pinkney (VPB-205) and his artwork . . . . . . . . . . . . . . . 157  
Pilots F. Dickey, VPB-21, and Lee Orsak, VPB-21 . . . . . . . . . . . . 158  
Bob Shaw, VPB-21, crew 9, plane captain . . . . . . . . . . . . . . . 158  
Pilots B. J. Mountain, VPB-21, and P. E. Casey, VPB-21 . . . . . . . . . 159  
Burke, Kyle, and (?) of VPB-17 on Luzon June 1945 . . . . . . . . . . 159  
Lt. Joe Durda, VPB-21, PPC of crew 14 . . . . . . . . . . . . . . . . 160  
Bill Ferrall and a couple of his buddies from VPB-208 . . . . . . . . . 160  
ARM2c Harvey Herzog, VPB-18, gets his air medal . . . . . . . . . . . 161  
VPB-216's Bob Smith's plane headed home . . . . . . . . . . . . . . . 162  
VPB-27's E-2 flying over Golden Gate Bridge on a foggy morning . . . . 170  
The author today . . . . . . . . . . . . . . . . . . . . . . . . . . 172  
The author in 1945 . . . . . . . . . . . . . . . . . . . . . . . . . 172

# FOREWORD

*Seaplanes at War—A Treasury of Words and Pictures* is a one-of-a-kind pictorial walk through one aspect of World War II history. One can close his/her eyes and imagine him/herself assigned to one of the U.S. Navy patrol squadrons in the Pacific, flying a Martin PBM Mariner aircraft, affectionately known as a "big boat." You will find yourself immersed in the Pacific theater of operations right up until the end of the war. Many of our fathers, brothers, and close friends served with distinction during the Pacific war. Many didn't come home. This book will enable you to better understand what they went through in those days in faraway places with strange-sounding names.

Meet the aircrews who fought and died for our great nation, the ships (seaplane tenders) that supported our big boats, and the fanatical enemy that developed one of the biggest surprises of the war: the then-new idea (and reality) of the Japanese special attack forces—the kamikaze corps and other suicide squads.

Photographs reproduced in this book will reinforce and surround you with the historical account of the Navy's PBM patrol squadrons during World War II.

—Nevins A. Frankel ("U. S. Navy Patrol Squadrons")
Waldorf, Maryland, 1998
http://www.vpnavy.com

# PREFACE

The seaplane in this pictorial history—the PBM Mariner, manufactured by the Glenn L. Martin Company—served, with modifications, in various capacities during World War II . . . as a cargo carrier, for example. But its primary task was to function as a long-range patrol bomber in the patrol bombing squadrons (VPBs) and in the air-sea rescue squadrons (VH), familiarly known as Dumbos.

The original designation for the VPBs was simply VP (V for heavier than air, P for patrol). But in October 1944 the squadron designators were changed to VPB (V for heavier than air, P for patrol, B for bombing) because squadron orders soon included regular bombing tasks as well as other duties. In this book, I've used the designation VPB for all references to a given squadron, even though it was not officially the designation until October 1944.

There is an autobiographical side to this story too. I flew with one of the squadrons in this story. I was an aircrewman (a sailor aviator) in one of these "boats that fly." My first PBM book's title, *The Sailor Aviators*, is the best term I could come up with to describe the versatility of a seaplane's crew. Seaplane pilots were skilled beyond the usual piloting skills . . . seamanship was an integral part of their job, and the enlisted crew members had to develop seamanship skills also. I flew in Patrol Bombing Squadron 21 (VPB-21). Some of its story is included here.

Prior to joining the Navy I had little exposure outside the neighborhood where I grew up. A good deal of my knowledge of the world, as I recall, was gained through pictures . . . *National Geographic* and *Life* magazines being good examples. Pictures took me to places beyond my imagination and allowed me some understanding of places and things that I had never had an opportunity to see or visit.

So my motivation in putting this story together is simple. I wanted to do a visual tale as well as one with words. One that, unlike other books about seaplanes, would have a wider appeal to the audience that lived through the years of World War II, but also to those who were not alive or who were very young during this period. A story that would bring with immediacy through photos the "daily war" of a group of Navy aircrew personnel in the Pacific Ocean battleground. I hope this format will be particularly interesting to the younger generation—our children and grandchildren, who tend, as I did and still do, to get more from pictures than from the written word.

I also want this story to highlight the role of seaplanes, so they do not get lost in the annals of history.

I do not presume that I could write a scholarly treatise on this subject, as the broad complexities of that global war are beyond my skills. I am a storyteller, not an author. This story covers the time frame of December 1943 through September 1945.

These pictures were not commissioned by anyone. In fact, many were taken "under cover." Almost all are by nonprofessional photographers. They truly are candid shots. Because of the amount of time between the war and now, I have sometimes had to resort to photocopies.

Personal cameras were pretty much forbidden in the armed forces during World War II. (Now, over fifty years later, these photos have been declassified and are parts of private collections.) I hope these photos will present a new vision of the seaplane at war. Because a photograph captures an incident, a happening, forever. What better way is there to assure that the PBMs and the men who flew in them will have a place in naval aviation history?

The incidents captured in these photos are not all-inclusive, but are meant to be representative of the many actions of PBMs. It would be impossible to portray every significant incident during these years in one book. I hope these photos are an accurate portrayal of everyday life as I or anyone that was there remembers: the fear, the boredom, the devastation, and the harshness of war. They are meant to let the reader *see* what it was like, rather than just imagine from the written word what happened there.

But there are words in this book, too. These words, though minimal compared to the number of photos, are the words of individuals with powerful visual recollections.

We sailor aviators flew solo missions, a lot of which consisted of the boring surveillance of thousands of miles of ocean. But during those missions we never knew when we would become caught up in some heavy action against ships, submarines, aircraft, or ground targets. It is my hope that this books brings some of this uncertainty and danger back to my readers. For these experiences, and those of many other units in the U.S. armed forces in the 1940s, led to the comparative peace we all enjoy today.

—Donald H. Sweet
Ridgewood, New Jersey 1999

# A LETTER TO MY READERS

I think that, after fifty some years, a little trip back to the war in the Pacific may help people who do not know a lot about those days. The Japanese opened this war with smashing victories everywhere they wanted to, particularly at Pearl Harbor and in the western Pacific, the Indian Ocean, the Java Sea, and Singapore. The effect of these victories was unbelievable for the U.S. public, many of whom thought the war would last but a few weeks.

Probably the hardest hit were the old-time Navy men. They were definitely taken aback by the clever tactics of the Japanese, who did away with any thought of a battleship war and forced our hand by using aircraft carriers as the offensive front line.

The airplane, in many instances, replaced the sixteen-inch guns of the big ships. For the first time, seaplanes played a major role in this war. This changeover in mentality did not go down particularly well with the old-timers, as noted, but the transition was made, and our carriers and seaplanes became the major factor in the Pacific war.

To tell a story such as this is difficult because there are so many people involved, so many years have passed, and our memories are dimming with time. Many of the official reports and daily diaries kept are inaccurate, because people see things differently in the heat of the battle. If all the airplanes that were claimed as destroyed *were in* fact destroyed, for example, there would not have been any air force left for either of the combatants.

So it is at times hard to bring complete objectivity to writing about a subject that is so vast and confusing. More eloquent words than I have used were spoken by Artemus L. Gates, Assistant Secretary of the Navy.

In 1945, upon his return from a Pacific tour, Gates announced that Martin Mariner seaplanes "were more in contact with the enemy than any other type of naval aircraft." The Mariners, he said, had "landed at their sea bases within a day or so of the first landings at Morotai, Mindoro, Leyte, and Lingayen g1

Gulf. Later, the Mariners became the 'eyes' in the Iwo Jima area because land planes based in the Marianas were too far way to provide more than meager coverage. Seaplane squadrons, the Navy says, flew twenty-one percent of all the Navy's night-action sorties throughout the entire war (Associated Press 1945)."

—Donald H. Sweet

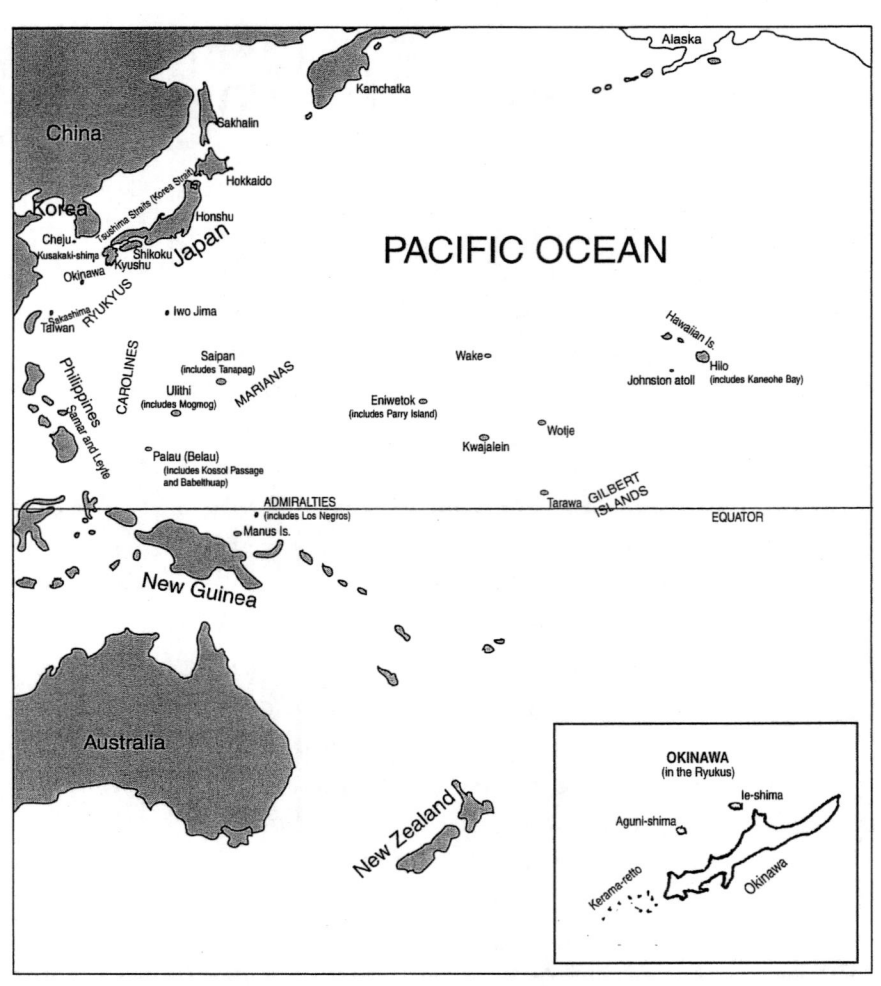

# THE ISLANDS

*Parry Island shortly after naval bombardment in 1944. (Art Kennedy photo collection)*

LEFT: *Kerama-retto gardens—a good place to catch a snake! (Source unknown)*

BELOW: *Babelthuap Island, in the Palaus. U.S. troops did not invade, due to 10,000 Japanese soldiers garrisoned here. Daily air patrols ensured that they remained cut off from Japanese resupply. PBMs had alert buoy watches at the Kossol Passage seadrome, about three or four miles from the island. (B. J. Mountain photo collection)*

# ISLANDS OVERVIEW

The Pacific Ocean battleground was huge. The Pacific covers some one third of the earth's total surface. It is usually thought of in terms of the north Pacific and the south Pacific—pretty logical—with the equator as the dividing line. It covers an amazing 64 million square miles. There are some thirty thousand islands, the largest of which are Japan, Taiwan, the Philippines, New Guinea, New Zealand, and Indonesia. Our sailor aviators became most familiar with the smaller islands like Saipan, Babelthuap, Mogmog, Okinawa, the various islands of the Philippines, and the islands in the Dutch East Indies.

I often felt as if we of VPB-21 had seen them all, but our view was really comparatively infinitesimal. I certainly gained at least a *sense* of the Pacific's magnitude, though, as I spent five hundred hours flying over it.

I always thought a lot of us were disappointed that we saw no women who looked like the Dorothy Lamours or Esther Williamses of Hollywood's islands. As a matter of fact, the islands we occupied were far from the tropical paradises portrayed by Hollywood directors. A description of Saipan in the Marianas, from a Navy manual, for the edification of servicemen stationed there, should give readers a picture of how it really was:

> *Saipan is an island ringed by sea life: sharks, barracuda, poisonous sea snakes, anemones, razor-sharp coral, polluted waters, poisonous fish, and giant clams that could shut on a man like a bear trap. The joys of life ashore include a variety of things: leprosy, typhus, filariasis, yaws, typhoid, dengue fever, dysentery, saber grass, insects of many varieties, snakes, and giant lizards. The rules are basic: Don't eat anything growing on the island, don't drink the water, and don't approach the inhabitants* (Bureau of Aeronautics 1944).

*Two more that will never fly again for Hirohito. (B. J. Mountain photo collection)*

LEFT: *The original john on Parry Island—a fly's paradise! (Art Kennedy photo collection)*

BELOW: *Our modern tent city on Parry Island, 1945. (Source unknown)*

Few of the central Pacific islands were more than coral atolls, while the southwest Pacific islands tended to have a different topography. Despite similar temperatures, the southwest Pacific had trees and hills and mountains, all on islands much larger than those in the central Pacific. The central Pacific islands were mainly flat, with little vegetation. We all talked about the weather as if it were also an enemy. It was: the heat could be unbearable, whether aboard ship or on some of the islands.

Many of the southwest Pacific islands are very sparsely populated. Most of the PBM activity in this area was launched from seaplane tenders, and a good deal of their flying activity was done as Black Cat missions (low-level nighttime flights).

Kwajalein, which is the largest coral atoll in the world, is some 2,415 miles southwest of Hawaii. It was invaded and taken over from the Japanese in February 1944, and became a major naval base for the Americans.

Eniwetok was a large atoll with a twenty-five-mile-wide lagoon and some forty islands. The major islands were Eniwetok Island itself, Parry Island, where the PBM squadrons were based, and Engebi on the opposite side of the lagoon.

Saipan was the largest of the fifteen islands comprising the Marianas archipelago. Saipan was taken over by the Americans in July 1944, along with the major Japanese seaplane base at

*Parry Island "sanitation department" sign:* WHEN USING BEACH AS A HEAD, GO AS NEAR TO THE WATER AS POSSIBLE. *(Source unknown)*

Tanapag Harbor on the northwest side of the island. Tanapag became the busiest American seaplane base in the Pacific, other than those in Hawaii. Saipan was the first island many of us saw that had a "skyline." It had a spine of hills running the length of the island instead of the typical flat, nondescript coral atoll.

One operating area I will never forget is Palau, a group of about a hundred islands, part of the Caroline Islands. The largest island of the group is Babelthuap, which is about a thousand miles southwest of Saipan and about a thousand miles southeast of Manila, Philippines.

Babelthuap is a hilly island with heavy vegetation—like the ones we visualize when we think of the tropics. At its northern end is Kossol Passage, where our seadrome was located, basically an open-sea area used to park seaplanes. There were still thousands of Japanese on many of the Palau islands after we took Peleliu and Angaur by October 1944, the two most useful islands because of their airstrips. Babelthuap, for example, so near to our seadrome at Kossol Passage, was held by 10,000 Japanese. (The U.S. command bypassed heavily held islands that it didn't need, on the theory that cutting such islands off was just as effective, and saved American lives.)

Ulithi Atoll, about halfway between the Philippines and Guam, was a major staging base for future action against the Japanese. But it is most fondly remembered by sailors as the place they went ashore (Mogmog Island) for a couple of hours, to relax with a few cold beers! It also became a favorite target area for Japanese submarines.

*Three of the VPB-25 guys looking over a downed Japanese float plane in Leyte Gulf, Philippines. (Source unknown)*

*Suicide cliff on Saipan, January 1945. (B. J. Mountain photo collection)*

Iwo Jima has the unfortunate history of being one of the bloodiest battles of World War II in the Pacific theater. The prize was the airfields that provided an emergency landing area for the B-29s making regular daily raids on Japan itself. Iwo was a terribly bloody battle in volcanic soil resulting in the loss of some twenty thousand Japanese lives and five thousand U.S. Marines. It took thirty bloody days to secure the island, which had a maze of tunnels and hidden gun positions like nothing encountered before by the Marines.

VPB-19 attempted to operate from waters near Iwo Jima, but the lack of even the semblance of a seadrome prevented any real activity and the venerable mariners gave up after about a week of frustration and many damaged planes.

Okinawa, the last island battleground of the Pacific war, was mountainous, very hot, and extremely prone to typhoons. It is a large island, some sixty miles long and up to eleven miles wide. The Okinawa area was the scene of the most horrendous battle of the Pacific war. The kamikazes became a major factor there. The overall casualty statistics were staggering: the United States had 15,500 killed and 51,000 wounded. The Japanese suffered 131,000 dead, including 42,000 civilians.

Kerama-retto, a few miles south of the main island of Okinawa, was the home base seadrome for the PBMs that operated out of Okinawa.

The islands we knew best were a mixture of topographies. For example, Johnston Island was two sandbars in a coral reef, eight hundred miles west-southwest of Pearl Harbor. It was just big enough for a lengthy landing strip and a seaplane base. It served as a stopover for almost all the planes going west to the combat zone, and then again when they were going back home. The Philippines were the other extreme—quite large.

Wake Island, some 480 miles east of Eniwetok, was one of the many islands bypassed by U.S. forces. Since it had a strong garrison of Japanese troops there, the U.S. command decided to simply cut it off from Japanese forces instead of taking the island militarily. Regular (daily) air patrols were made to Wake to ensure that the Japanese could not resupply their stranded troops there. It was the most heavily gunned island in the central Pacific. According to the best information I could find (Naval intelligence), the Japanese had some 350 guns there, from 20-mm to 5-inch, plus some heavy antiaircraft guns.

## MOVING ON

The Marianas operation was in many ways a great learning experience for all our sailor aviators. Plans were put into motion with VPB-202, -16, -216, -17, and -21 leading the way. This was part of the plan to invade the Philippines. These PBM squadrons provided patrol, bombing, and photo reconnaissance missions to support this assault. As would become the pattern, seaplane squadrons were the first air power to establish themselves at the invasion target.

After the Marianas were secured, PBMs moved into the Palau Islands in the northern part of the Caroline island group.

*The ramp and a burned-out Japanese hangar at Tanapag seaplane base, Tanapag, Saipan. (Source unknown)*

*Iwo Jima's anchorage. The hole in the cliff (right of center in photo) was a tunnel for a small piece of artillery. (George Lindberg photo collection)*

Kossol Passage, the open-sea area northeast of the main island of Babelthuap in the Palaus, was to be the seadrome. This seadrome was officially established on September 16, 1944. The arrival of the first group of PBMs was greeted by exploding mines, as mine-clearing operations were still under way. This pattern continued through the battle for Okinawa.

## THE SOUTHWEST PACIFIC

Major activity by the PBM squadrons in the southwest Pacific was primarily from the Philippines; Lingayen and Leyte gulfs, Manila Bay, Palawan, and Tawitawi. This was a bit different, inasmuch as there was a fair amount of land, as opposed to the endless ocean I was used to. I am glad I was in the central Pacific. As much as I hate heat, I hate humidity all the more. When I hear about two hundred thirty inches of rain on places like New Guinea, it's too much. The heat, which could be debilitating, also brought about skin problems and all of us in the Pacific remember the purple medication they painted you with. If it was hot ashore, it was brutal aboard ship, but at least there were showers, so you could be comfortable for a while. When based ashore, most of us counted on the daily downpours to provide fresh water while we stood naked in them.

Funafuti Island, in the southwest Pacific, posed some unusual problems, as VPB-20 discovered one fine morning. The water was often like glass, and the hull of the planes couldn't break from the surface. They even tried using other planes to stir up the water by crisscrossing the lagoon. That was unusual, as the base was in reality a Naval Air Transport Service seaplane base. Fortunately, it was not an everyday problem.

## BACK TO THE PHILIPPINES

When the United States began their return to the Philippines, one of the first moves was to get some PBM squadrons there to relieve the PBY squadrons who had served long tours in the southwest Pacific. PBM squadrons VPB-20 and -25 were the first to begin operations there, beginning with the invasion of Leyte in October 1944.

As more of the Philippines came under the control of the

*Kerama-retto on a quiet afternoon, May 1945. (Lee Roy Way photo collection)*

Americans, VPB-17, VPB-28, and VH-4 moved in. Missions were begun on a large scale against he Japanese in the southwest Pacific.

## THE CENTRAL PACIFIC

I honestly believe that a poll of central Pacific Navy veterans would show that the best island was Mogmog in the Ulithi Atoll. This was a major fleet recreation area. It had two real assets: cold beer and solid ground for basketball courts, softball fields, and such.

The beer was one of the worst I've ever tasted—called Acme or something similar, from Washington state. But to thirsty sailors it was the nectar of the gods. There were more drunks per square yard there than probably any other place I have ever been. And fights!!! All it took was "Hey, Mac, what ship are you on?" and *pow!* someone was on their rear end. But it was a little relief for shipboard sailors who may have been "out there" for months and months and needed to let off some steam.

*Kerama-retto with the AVP USS Mackinac in the foreground and four Mariners in the background. What a lovely way to spend an evening! (Lee Roy Way photo collection)*

*Iwo Jima's D-day (February 1945), with Mt. Surabachi dominating the landscape. VPB-19 flew from here for a week, and then gave up because there was no good seadrome area at Iwo Jima. The seven faint dots on the right of the photo are Mariners tied to buoys. (George Lindberg photo collection)*

TOP: *Three VPB-205 armed guards heading for a beer on Parry Island . . . sure they'll get their ration. April 1945. Left to right: (?), George Pinnell, Sam Clinton.*

BOTTOM: *Wake Island just prior to final surrender in 1945. VPB-21 dropped leaflets with the terms of surrender onto the island. (Jim Guay photo collection)*

TOP: *Waikiki Beach in front of the Royal Hawaiian Hotel. (Don Sweet photo collection)*

BOTTOM: *MGM's western Pacific franchise—Parry Island, Eniwetok Atoll. (Source unknown)*

TOP: *VPB-216: Housecleaning day at Parry Island. (Dick Agnello photo collection)*

BOTTOM: *Up, up, and away from Tanapag to Yap today: VPB-216 taking off for the day's mission. (Doc Doherty photo collection)*

TOP: *Los Negros in the Admiralties—the native huts looked better than those tents we used!* (Don Kramer photo collection)

BOTTOM: *The ramp at Hilo, Hawaii—a great R&R spot!* (Source unknown)

16    Seaplanes at War

TOP: *This bike was a "gift" from OOD (officer of the day) at Kaneohe, Hawaii. It was originally with a motorbike that was "requisitioned," then returned to OOD prior to VPB-21 crew 1's leaving Kaneohe Bay. (Source unknown)*

BOTTOM: *VPB-21's ground crew. Left to right, back row: Hipps, Neuman, Jones. Front row: Gallagher, Volpe. (Merlin Jones photo collection)*

18    Seaplanes at War

FACING PAGE, TOP AND BOTTOM: *Two of the latest "Maytag C3 model" washing machines on Saipan (top), and on Parry Island, Eniwetok (bottom). (Source unknown)*

BELOW: *Laundry and housekeeping day at Saipan, and some of the guys from VPB-216. (Source unknown)*

*"Suicide Gap" at Kerama-retto, with kamikazes on the attack. The explosion in the gap, though shaped like an atomic bomb's, is from a "regular" bomb. (Source unknown)*

# THE PLANES

*One of VPB-21's PBM-3Ds taking off from Eniwetok en route to Saipan and Palau. (Fred Dickey photo collection)*

## OVERVIEW

The actual beginning of the story of the Martin Mariner PBM in the Pacific war is January 1944 in the Gilbert Islands, at Tarawa, the site of one of the bloodiest battles of the Pacific war and certainly one never to be forgotten in the annals of the U.S. Marine Corps. Tarawa was the first base of operations for PBMs in the Pacific battle zone. VPB-202, flying PBM-3Ds, was the first to be deployed to the Pacific (to Tarawa) in January 1944.

## THE POLITICS OF WAR

A real issue in this period of the war was the feud between the Army's General Douglas MacArthur and the Navy's admirals over the direction the war should be taking. MacArthur argued long and hard for taking the Philippines first. He attempted to use the horrendous casualty rate on Tarawa as a tool to take control over the direction of the war in the Pacific. (The Marines had 3,301 casualties; 1,000 deaths. The Japanese had 4,836 troops

*"Up, up and away. We are off to visit Iwo again today." (Don Sweet photo collection)*

there, and 4,690 of them were killed!) MacArthur was quoted as stating, "Give me central direction of the war in the Pacific and I will be in the Philippines in ten months" (according to an Associated Press report in 1943).

But the insistent arguments of the USAAF (United States Army Air Force) about acquiring bases in the Marianas for their new long-range bombers, the B-29s, to bomb Japan proper, won out. The main thrust of the war then was not to go up through the Philippines, but rather through the central Pacific—the Marshall Islands and then on to the Marianas.

The scuttlebutt (gossip) was that the Philippines only became important because MacArthur made it a crusade of his and wanted them to be under U.S. control. Supposedly, it was said by many knowledgeable people at the time that the war might have been shorter if the Philippines could have been bypassed as were many other islands in the Pacific.

Before going any further let me identify the patrol bombing squadrons of this story: VPB-16, -17, -18, -19, -20, -21, -22, -25, -26, -27, -28, -202, -205, -208, and -216; and the air-sea rescue squadrons were VH-1, -2, -3, -4, -5, and -6.

As noted above, the central Pacific offensive and the combat initiation against the Japanese for the PBM began in the Gilbert Islands in January 1944. Once the Gilberts were taken, the Marshalls became the next target. Kwajalein fell first, and then the move was made on Eniwetok in late February. With the fall of Eniwetok, the first major break in the Japanese line of defense through the central Pacific had been made. During this same period, Truk, a major Japanese naval base, was attacked and effectively neutralized without having to be invaded. That caused what had been the key Japanese naval base in the central Pacific to be moved to Palau, in the Carolines. The Marianas now became the prime target, and Saipan was invaded in June.

The Marianas Islands, Saipan, Tinian, and Guam in particular, were strategic locations for the Americans as they had been for the Japanese. The Japanese had used them as a major staging area for naval operations, and the Americans wanted them too. For this progression of airfields, ever nearer to Japan, would allow the United States to begin bombing the Japanese homeland.

In early 1945 Iwo Jima, in the Bonins, was taken, and we achieved the emergency airfield we wanted. The mainland of Japan became a daily target for our bombers, with their new safety valve, Iwo Jima. Then on April 1, 1945, the icing on the cake: the invasion of Okinawa, which gave us a base of operations within about three hundred fifty miles of the Japanese mainland. This was to be the crown in the PBM operations. This four-and-a-half-month battle, the costliest of the Pacific war, was real proof of the value of the venerable Mariner. This battle also exposed the U.S. fleet to the kamikazes in untold numbers. It is estimated that some two thousand kamikaze attacks were launched during the battle for the island of Okinawa.

## THE PBM COMES OF AGE

When the war started, the Navy only had six first-line aircraft carriers in the fleet. The *Lexington* was lost during the battle of the Coral Sea in May 1942, the *Wasp* off Guadalcanal in September 1942, and the *Hornet* went down in October. The *Saratoga* (twice) and the *Enterprise* were torpedoed in 1942. The *Enterprise* then was the only operational carrier after some emergency repairs.

This shortage of carriers was one of the reasons the PBY Catalina was so valuable early in the war as the only Navy patrol bomber. These truly were "the eyes of the fleet" (*Must We* 1997). You can't talk about seaplanes without giving top billing to Consolidated's PBY Catalina. It has to be one of the great airplanes of all time. The PBY-1 first flew in September 1936 and

*VPB-21's V-5 plane, a PBM-5, on patrol just east of the Japanese coast, which can be seen in the background. (Norb Ullman photo collection)*

24   Seaplanes at War

there are later models still flying today, in 1998. It performed incredibly in World War II, from the usual patrols to dive-bombing, torpedo attacks, Dumbo (air-sea rescue) work, and above all as "Black Cats," flying low-level night missions. The name Black Cats evolved from the practice of painting PBYs all black so they could fly more safely at low altitude at night (without being seen). The PBY was very instrumental in helping hold the line several times early in the war.

So too did some PBM squadrons paint their Mariners all black, and install flame suppressors on the engine exhaust stacks. These tactics effectively made the PBMs almost invisible at night.

The third major seaplane employed by the Navy in World War II was Consolidated's Coronado, a large four-engine seaplane. It never quite proved itself, so the PBM became the backbone for the Navy.

## THE MARTIN MARINER

The PBM Martin Mariner arrived on the scene at the perfect time and was an ideal replacement for the PBY, although the PBY continued to fly throughout the war. Following in the PBY's footsteps, the PBM, I feel, became a more effective plane as it got more combat exposure. It was a tough plane, very sound structurally, as evidenced by how it just about always got you home despite many incidents of severe combat damage or damage from the ever-dangerous sea. It was admirably suited to

ABOVE: *A PBM-5's cockpit. (Bill Ferrall photo collection)*

BELOW: *The navigator's and flight engineer's stations of a PBM-5. (Bill Ferrall photo collection)*

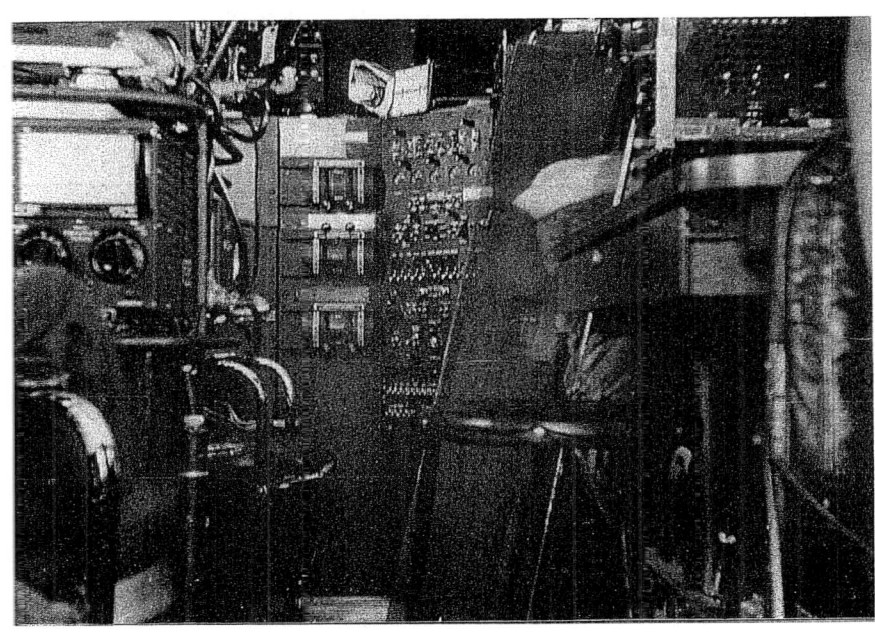

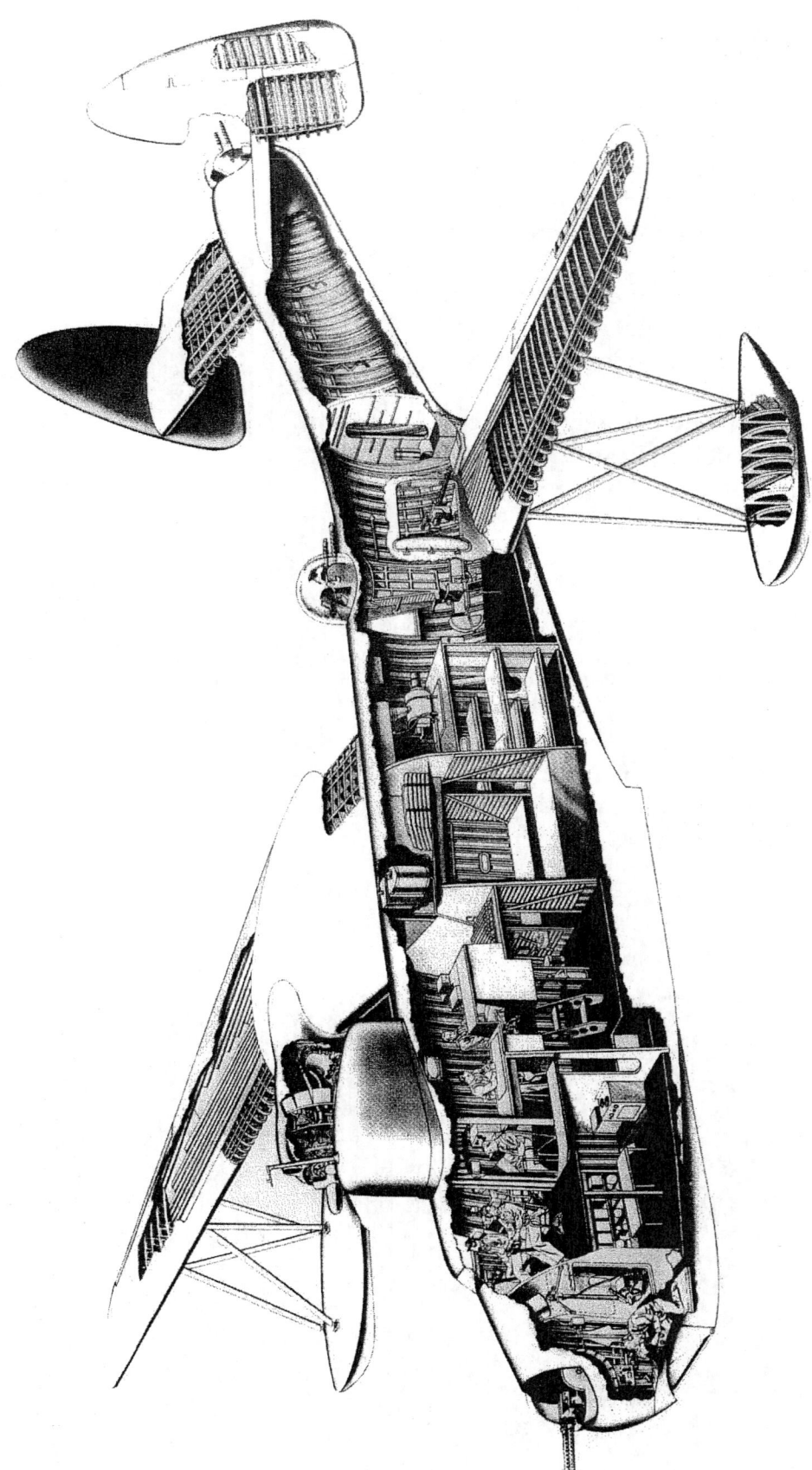

*A cutaway picture of the PBM-5 showing the five sections of its fuselage quite clearly. (Signal Publications photo collection)*

the Pacific war environment, being pretty much of a self-contained fighting unit.

The Mariner, which looked like a cross between a boat and a plane, had the needed firepower, the load-carrying capacity, and a hull that allowed open-sea landings and takeoffs under almost impossible sea conditions. At a number of the locations where PBMs operated, just the daily routine of takeoff and landing was like operating from the open sea. For example, the Mariners based at Kossol Passage in the Palaus and at Kerama-retto in the Ryukyus were kept wherever safe water was available, which often happened to be in areas of comparatively rough waters. No other planes could have withstood the battering the Mariners took in these "harbors."

It was often said by PBM crew members that their biggest enemy was the sea and the weather. To get the real feel for this big bird, see the cutaway picture of a PBM-5.

## THE MARIANAS AND PALAUS

As already noted, the Marianas operation was in many ways a great learning experience for all our sailor aviators. It was the first multi-squadron operation by PBMs in the Pacific. After the Marianas were secured, the next move was to take the Mariners to the Palaus. (It should be noted that in October 1944 squadron designators for the VP squadrons were changed to VPB, to show that they were also now bombing squadrons.)

The pickings were awfully good for the squadrons in the southwest Pacific area, as attested to by commendations issued to VPB-20 and VPB-28:

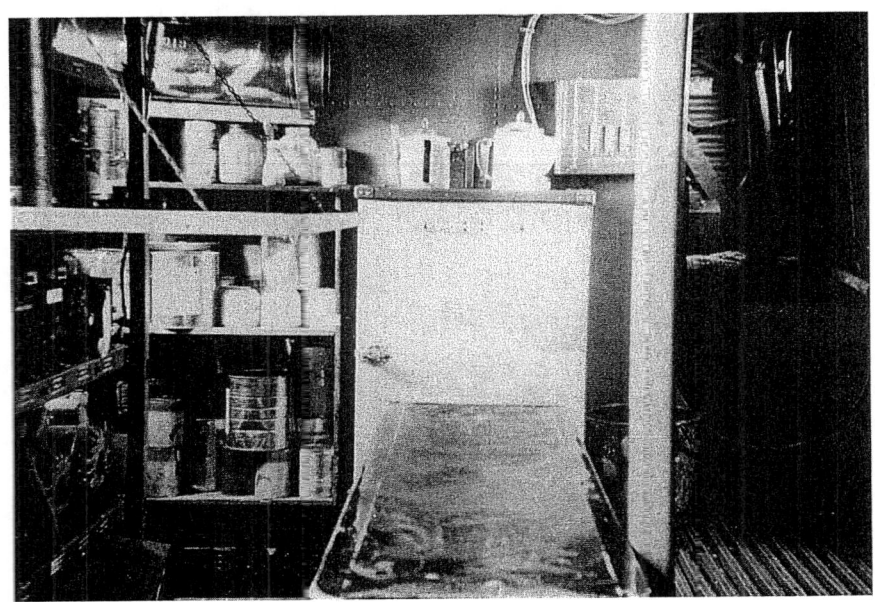

BELOW: *A PBM-5's galley. (Bill Ferrall photo collection)*

*Consolidated's PB2Y Coronado from VPB-13—"the big baby with a soft belly"—coming aboard a tender at Kerama-retto. (Bill Ferrall photo collection)*

*For outstanding heroism in action against enemy Japanese force in Indo-China, and Netherlands East Indies from November 1, 1944, to June 1, 1945. Engaged in night-and-day offensive searches, night convoy coverage, and bombing missions throughout this period, sinking 42,000 tons and inflicting serious damage on more than 82,000 tons of Japanese shipping. Individually heroic and aggressive, the pilots and aircrewmen flew in support of the Tarakan Island, Brunei Bay, and Balikpapan operations, not only providing effective protection for amphibious forces proceeding from the staging area, but also carrying out low-level coastal and river armed reconnaissance. Their perseverance, high standards of achievement, and unwavering devotion to duty reflect the highest credit upon Patrol Bombing Squadron 20 and the United States Naval Service.*

*—James Forrestal
Secretary of the Navy*

Admiral Kincaid commended VPB-28 on their achievements against Japanese shipping:

*It is with the satisfaction that I forward the following message from the Commander of the Seventh Fleet: "Congratulations on the record you have achieved in the last three months. You have hit the enemy many times where it hurts the most. Your perseverance and devotion to duty reflect the highest credit on VPB-28 and the pilots and aircrewmen who participated in these actions."*

ABOVE: *One of the real heros of this story, the Black Cat PBM of VPB-28—a cat with long claws. See scoreboard below cockpit window. (Bob Van Trieste photo collection)*

BELOW: *One of the original Black Cats—a PBY-5A Catalina from VPB-54. The crew is awaiting transport to a tender in Kerama-retto. (Fred Dickey photo collection)*

ABOVE: *A PBM-5, with its JATO mechanism mounted on its wings, tied up to buoy at Saipan. (George Lindberg photo collection)*

BELOW: *A good shot of a JATO takeoff at Kerama-retto. Just as the JATO fires, the overloaded PBM-5 leaps into the air. (VH-3 photo collection)*

## JATO

JATO (jet-assisted takeoff), which became readily available about April of 1945, was of great assistance. As an example, VH-3, flying PBM-3s, made JATO takeoffs in an average of nine seconds. I heard from some of the aircrewmen in VH-3 that at times the plane had previously been thrown off rough water before they achieved flying speed; this could happen in wind conditions as low as forty knots. The power of the JATO, plus the engines, now helped keep the plane airborne long enough to allow the required air speed to be attained, and off they went.

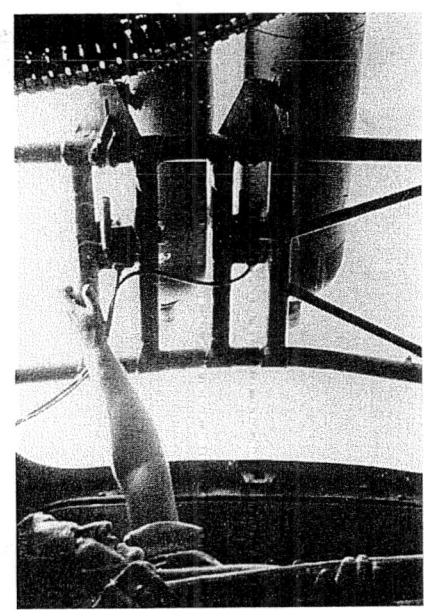

ABOVE: *Mariner E-2 of VPB-27. Bob Dorrance, AMM, just after takeoff, with expended JATO bottles. (Bill Ferrall photo collection)*

## BIG BIRD

The PBM was a big airplane, with a wingspan of 118 feet and a length of 79 feet. It had a maximum weight of 58,000 pounds. Armament consisted of eight .50-caliber M-2 machine guns. There were two each in the bow, the deck, and tail turrets, all electrohydraulic-controlled with Mark VIII electric gunsights. And the two waist guns, also .50-caliber M-2s, had hydraulic controls or could be used manually. This armament was later supplemented by two .30-caliber machine guns, one in each of the bow hatches. A bomb load of 4,000 pounds (bombs, depth charges, or mines) was carried in bomb bays in the aft end of the engine nacelles. Also, two Mark XIII torpedoes could be carried, one under each wing, between the hull and the engine nacelle.

## IT'S A LONG RUNWAY

A real coincidence, just as I was composing this page, I received one of many letters I get regularly from old PBM crew members. This was from Jim Kraker, who joined VPB-21 after I had been rotated back home. He related an incident at Okinawa while

BELOW: *A VPB-19 JATO takeoff from Iwo Jima, February 1945. (George Lindberg photo collection)*

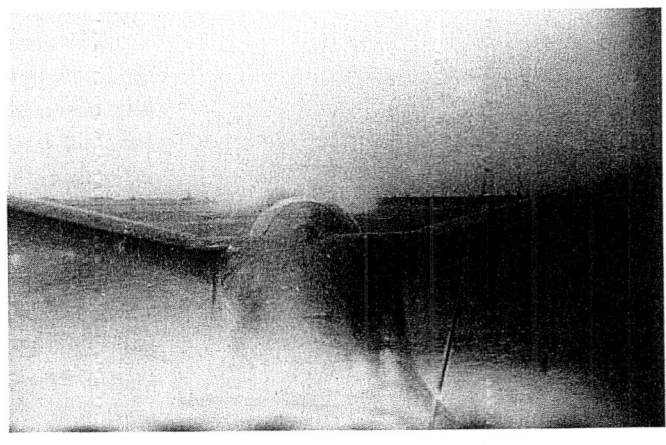

escaping a typhoon. The whole squadron was ordered back to Saipan and Jim takes it from there:

> *We took the whole squadron off from Buckner Bay, plane after plane, like clockwork, even though the swells had increased to twenty-seven feet before the last plane, which was mine, took off. We did it with no JATO. My run was five miles in the trough before I had enough speed to ignore wind direction and could climb up the swell to the crest and then take off. My copilot and I were soaked with sea water coming in through the windows, which wouldn't remain shut....*

Hard to believe? Not if you spent any time at Kossol Passage or Kerama-retto. Just another example of sailor aviator skills.

## THE ART OF BUOY MAKING

A really good, albeit tongue-in-cheek, example of the buoy-making skills required to be a sailor aviator is this one, written by Lt. Charles Atkinson, PPC of Crew 4 in VPB-21.

> *This is not intended to make an expert buoy maker of the reader, but it is a treatise on recognizing the problems of buoy making and of coping with them sanely.... All you have to do is taxi your plane up to an object and tie your bowline to it. It is this sheer simplicity that pulls the wool over one's eyes.... Naval Air Station Key West affords us a revolting example of how the elements can team up against a pilot in his quest of a buoy and send him off, calling his plane vulgar names like* Blowhard *and threatening to turn in his water wings.*
>
> *At that coral reef, people once made their living by causing ships to run aground and then looting the derelicts. But the law stopped that. However, there have been more seaplanes run aground since the law than ships previous to it. The current— always the opposite direction indicated by the sign on the beach (placed there by Key Westers)—is invariably against the wind. If you head into the wind, the current will send you sailing past the buoy on the step. If you head into the current, the wind will sail you by, likewise. In such a case, it is obvious that the desired condition is to have a fast and brave bowman. He might lose an arm trying, but after all, he gets sea pay.*
>
> *The obvious problem is to be at the buoy, going slowly enough for the bowman to pick up the buoy and make it fast to your plane's snubbing post with the bowline. To some bowmen this means come to a full stop and stay there while he finds a line in the after station and brings it forward. When in good humor, we call this type of bowman Butterfingers. But if you have a Butterfingers, it's advisable to send him up on the wing during the buoy making. That will get him out of the way and he might even fall off and drown.*
>
> *After the bowman takes at least two half-hitches around the snubbing post, it's time to yell, "Cut 'em." When the flight engineer has replied "Both engines in idle cutoff, sir," you may, if you like—and most pilots do like—shove both throttles wide open. This gives you the*

*mission-accomplished feeling. But it may send you away from the buoy and leave part of your plane there, too.*

*Of course, there are several theories on what to do if you miss the buoy. The one we encourage the least is to cover the eyes and recite the Lord's prayer. This usually ends in disaster, even for those who go to church every Sunday. If it looks as if the odds are against getting away without a hole or total disintegration of the plane, cut the engines and drop the anchor—not the buoy hook—then say the Lord's prayer while the crew closes all watertight doors and breaks out the bilge pump. If the plane stops before you hit anything, your worries about making the buoy are over* (Atkinson 1944).

## ALONE AND DANGEROUS

Patrol missions were almost always alone, long, and dangerous, lasting ten to thirteen hours, and at times even longer. As a pilot would tell you, flying over vast expanses of the ocean void of any landmarks required a high degree of piloting, as well as navigational, skill. Flying skills were tested to the ultimate, because flying over the ocean often meant a fair amount of flying

*Singling up at buoy, getting ready to cast off and taxi out for takeoff. (Fred Dickey photo collection)*

through tropical stormfronts, which caused violent wind shifts, drenching rains, and severe downdrafts to challenge the crews.

The Black Cats faced another problem: during their night flying at low altitude they were often completely at the mercy of their radar, as nothing was visible to the naked eye.

## OUR WORST ENEMY

The weather, as mentioned, was in some ways our worst enemy. The Pacific Ocean storms, with the exception of tornadoes, are the worst Mother Nature can conjure up. When you are on the ocean or flying over it, these storms can be vicious and there aren't many places to hide. There was another danger that is not given much thought: when a storm kicked up, the planes at buoy often took a beating from the boats bringing relief crews or food to the plane. They banged into the planes, damaging, often seriously, the hulls and rudders.

As noted, a critical skill for the crews was making the buoy (tying up to the buoy). In a sense, the buoy became home base while overseas. Pacific Mariner squadrons seldom had their planes ashore or on the tender, so the buoy was very important.

Even when coming ashore or onto a tender, a buoy came into play. So it was a regular job anytime the plane was moved. A big assist in making the buoy were the sea anchors, which were made of canvas material shaped into a cone and attached to a metal ring. These anchors were about three feet in diameter with a six- to ten-foot line attached for deploying, and then for tripping when no longer needed. They were our brakes. As we taxied to the ramp, or when making a buoy, one of these anchors could be deployed from the port or starboard waist hatch as needed, to slow the plane and assist in steering.

## BUOY WATCH: A WAY OF LIFE

Buoy watch was a way of life for the crews. It did have a serious side, as there had been occasions where Japanese swam out into the seadromes with hand grenades, in hopes of blowing up a plane at its buoy. Thus, a good deal of the time they had us on guard on the plane, in good weather and bad. We all got our sea legs this way! For such watches, it was standard operating procedure to always have a skeleton crew on board, twenty-four hours a day. At least one pilot and four enlisted men were there, serving as armed guards, and ready to move the plane if necessary.

Communication between plane and tender was by blinker

*Relief crews arriving at a plane at buoy. (B. J. Mountain photo collection)*

light, and each crew member was drilled in Morse code so that he could communicate with the ship.

The plane was occasionally on the ramp, if ramps were available at a seadrome. There was no landing gear on the Mariner, so portable beaching gear was utilized. This gear consisted of two sets of tandem wheels for main gear and a smaller set for the rear of the plane. Each had its own flotation device to facilitate getting it from the ramp to the plane by the beaching crew.

The wheels were attached in the water, then a tractor could tow the plane up onto the ramp. When ready to launch the Mariner back into the water, the tractor was attached to the plane's rear. The tractor then used its brakes and inched the plane down the ramp until the Mariner was floating in the water. Once in the water, the Mariner's temporary wheels were removed and pulled ashore.

Plane watch was also necessary when a plane was on the ramp. At Saipan, for example, there were eight Japanese soldiers killed in the ramp area of the seaplane base and one was captured after they were discovered trying to forage for food.

Planes had to be ready on a minute's notice—and they all took a regular beating in the rough water, particularly on takeoffs and landings. Refueling and minor maintenance—such as tightening bolts, studs, and wires—were therefore needed regularly. PBM mechanics, whether in PBM crews or on tenders, worked to keep them in continual tip-top shape, ready for use. Ammunition and other ordnance were kept loaded at all times.

Rough water made some of the more mundane tasks quite difficult and, at times, dangerous. Fueling could be particularly dangerous. My experience was that most of the time, overseas, we fueled from a bowser boat—a floating gasoline tanker. When

*Eniwetok, September 1944. Ever-constant engine maintenance being performed on the Wright Model R-2600-22 14-cylinder engine by T. P. Gengo, AMM3c, and C. E. Aldrich, AMM3c, flight engineers of Combat Air Crew 13 of Squadron VPB-17. (L. H. Roberts photo collection)*

the plane was on the beach, we usually fueled from a tanker truck.

Thinking back, as I often do, I have to say that takeoffs and landings were always quite "interesting" in these underpowered and usually overloaded seaplanes.

Logistics problems made the value of the seaplane much greater. The invasion of Saipan was a prime example of what made the seaplane essential, as there was no airfield within a thousand miles. The PBM made itself invaluable by having the range to reach American support bases in the Marshalls, some fifteen hundred miles away. It was also an island-hopping war, which was well suited to seaplanes, since they had a built-in runway.

## THE IRREPLACEABLE PATSUs

The level of activity in both the central and southwest Pacific kept the seaplane tenders busy. Many planes returned from missions with battle damage serious enough to warrant bringing the plane aboard immediately for repairs. Battle damage, in addition to the almost constant damage inflicted by the rough waters at the planes' anchorages, played real havoc with hulls, tail structures, and wingtip floats. The PATSUs (patrol aircraft service units) were great; they worked hard and often under extremely adverse conditions.

One of the mechanics in the USS *Chandeleur*'s PATSU made a really telling remark one day when he was out working on our plane. He said, "The length and frequency of flights and the saltwater environment take a real toll on the planes. . . . For every hour flown, a seaplane needs about three hours of maintenance. The worst part for me is the weather, as I have to hang on with one hand and work with the other from the rather flimsy engine stands attached to the wing of the plane." These mechanics deserve a great deal of the credit for working under very adverse conditions.

Another major problem were the kamikazes, particularly in the Philippines and Okinawa, who kept everyone on their toes with their constant attacks and, in some instances, just plain old nuisance flights during nighttime hours.

## THE "GOOD NEWS, BAD NEWS" MARINER

I would agree that flying in the PBM-3D was always an experience. The unreliable Curtiss-Wright engines (someone joked that it should be said, "They're manufactured by the Curtiss

Novelty Company") were a constant worry. Finally, in March of 1945 the original PBMs began to be replaced, and new PBM-5s arrived. The PBM-3D had been powered by two Curtiss-Wright R-2600-22 engines rated at 1900 horsepower, driving four-bladed propellers. The PBM-5 that replaced the -3D at the beginning of 1945 was equipped with better engines—the Pratt & Whitney R-2800-22, rated at 2100 horsepower. Also, maximum speed was 215 mph. Fuel capacity with drop bomb-bay tanks was 3,496 gallons; range was 2,300 to 2,400 miles per fueling.

The PBM, like a lot of war machines, performed many tasks that probably were not in the designers' minds when they built them. War has a way of utilizing things to its advantage and this plane may be a good example. Those of us who flew in them sometimes could not believe their capability and performance. There are many stories about the plane that tell how good it really was. For example, the time a plane made it back from patrol with three hundred bullet and shrapnel holes. Or the plane that made bombing runs on aircraft carriers. Or the ones that made open-sea landings in impossible seas. Story after story of forced single-engine operations for hundreds of miles. As Dick (Richard) Gingrich, a pilot in both VPB-27 and VPB-216 and chairman of the Mariner/Marlin Association, puts it, "It was never a sea burner; the plane flew low and slow. But it got you there! Pilots and crewmen alike grew to trust, yes to love, this gull-winged beauty. It was tough in difficult situations and if you treated her right, she would always bring you home to fly another day" (Mariner/Marlin Association 1993).

*VPB-21, crew 14, discussing an engine problem (at least one of the crew is!). (USS* Chandeleur *photo collection)*

## A LITTLE HUMOR GOES A LONG WAY

A well-known tradition in the armed forces is to name your plane. Reference is made here and there, in this book, to some of the names given to PBMs. Here is a list of just of few:

*Bachelor's Pad*
*Sexy Anna*
*Big Bertha*
*No Guts – No Glory*
*Passion Pit*
*Dinah Might*
*Ass-cend Don* (the author's turret)
*Miss Carriage*
*Charlot the Harlot*

*One of VH-3's PBM-5s just off the water. "Airborne in six seconds. Ain't JATO wonderful?" (Bill Ferrall photo collection)*

TOP: *Two PBM-5s that didn't survive a typhoon at Okinawa. (Source unknown)*

BOTTOM: *44. Another PBM-5 that didn't survive a typhoon at Okinawa. (Bill Ferrall photo collection)*

The Planes    39

*A PBM-3 launching from the ramp at NAS Key West, Florida. Note the beaching gear and the member of the beaching crew at the tail's wheel. (Source unknown)*

40   Seaplanes at War

*A bad night landing at Harvey Point, North Carolina—the beach, not the river. The entire crew escaped with minor cuts and bruises. (Dick Simms photo collection)*

*"Old Reliable" and the star of the show—another shot of the PBY Catalina (Black Cat). (Fred Dickey photo collection)*

TOP: *While VPB-27 E-2 is at buoy, the ordnance crew loads an aerial torpedo called Fido. (Bill Ferrall photo collection)*

BOTTOM: *Ready for any ship tonight! (Bill Ferrall photo collection)*

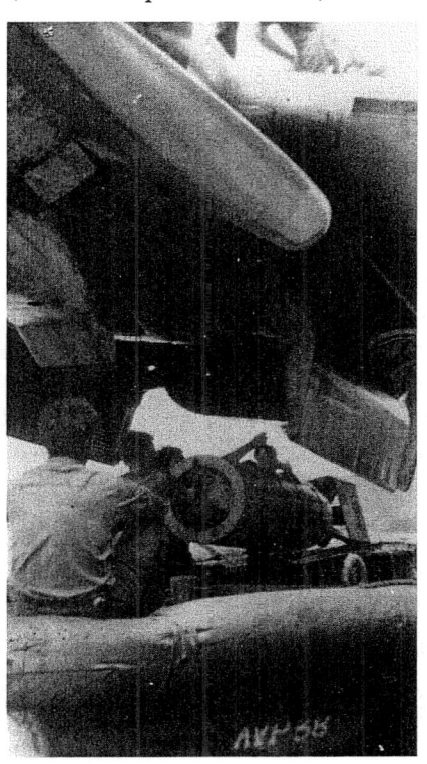

TOP: *Vance Kyle of Box 10, the "Mighty Ten-der" of VPB-17. The radar dome has been removed for some special work. (VPB-17 photo collection)*

BOTTOM: *The ever-busy ramp at NAS Kaneohe Bay, Hawaii. Planes look new, so probably they are heading west to the war. (Bill Ferrall photo collection)*

VPB-21's Victor 7, *Sexy Anna, after being all shot up in an attack on a Japanese convoy off Korea, barely made it back to Kerama-retto. (Fred Dickey photo collection)*

TOP: *A VPB-19 Mariner leaves Tanapag seadrome, Saipan, for Iwo Jima duty. Note JATO unit under port wing. (George Lindberg photo collection)*

BOTTOM: *A VPB-13 PB2Y Coronado just back from a sortie along the China coast. (Fred Dickey photo collection)*

TOP: *A 40mm shell went through the starboard wings of this Mariner but left little real damage. (Source unknown)*

BOTTOM: *VPB-21, crew 17 (Bob Smith, PPC), on their second tour to Pacific comes aboard the USS* Chandeleur *for some hull repair. (USS* Chandeleur *photo collection)*

The Planes 47

TOP: *VPB-216's Mariner fueled up and tied down at buoy at Saipan: "mission tomorrow." (USS* Chandeleur *photo collection)*

BOTTOM: *VPB-13's PB2Y5 taxis into Kerama-retto. (Fred Dickey photo collection)*

TOP: *A Harvey Point, North Carolina, plane on the ramp at NAS Key West, Florida. Temp duty for ASW school. (Bill Ferrall photo collection)*

BOTTOM: *V-2 of VPB-21, at buoy in Kerama-retto on a rare calm day. The USS* Chandeleur *is in the background. (Fred Dickey photo collection)*

*A PBM-3D coming aboard its tender by crane, for repair. "Easy does it, up and on." (Source unknown)*

*Once on board, the PBM-3 is secured diagonally to conserve deck space on the tender. (Source unknown)*

*VPB-16's plane No. 11 crosses paths with VPB-21's V6 in midstream between Saipan and Palau. (Don Sweet photo collection)*

# THE MEN AND THEIR SQUADRONS

*Purple Heart award ceremony, USS* Chandeleur. *"Suffer the young men the wounds of war." (USS* Chandeleur *photo collection)*

# THE MEN

## OVERVIEW

Again I turn to Dick Gingrich to put the perfect perspective on the subject of dedication. In his dedication to the book *Mariner/Marlin, Anywhere, Anytime*, he wrote, "They came from farms and factories, from high school halls and college campuses, from rugged seacoasts and rolling prairies. They were bright, adventurous young men. They were among the best America had to offer.

"In a short period of training in flight and ground school, in special technical schools dealing with mechanics, ordnance, and communications, they learned and honed their skills. They were brought together in combat aircrews and squadrons to perform what was regarded by many as the most boring and least exciting of all military aviation duties. However, as the accounts in the following pages reveal, the exact opposite of this often became the truth. When the occasions presented themselves, these valiant pilots and aircrewmen performed many acts of daring and heroism with great skill and courage. (Mariner/Marlin Association 1993)"

ABOVE: *Several of the stalwarts with a local Filipino young lady. (Source unknown)*

BELOW: *Not the Top of the Mark, but at least the booze is cold. . . . The O Club at Tanapag, Saipan. (Art Kennedy photo collection)*

## HEROES

"War makes many heroes, and I have known some. I do believe that no one is born a hero. A person becomes a hero when he does what he thinks is right for another human being(s) without

*Four of "Norm's bad boys" (VPB-21) on liberty in Honolulu, July 1944, at the University of Hawaii, trying to soak up some "intellectualism." (Don Kramer photo collection)*

hesitation. It really becomes a question of circumstances and timing. Heroes are made because there is no time to react to a situation with fear or terror. They are too busy acting on the situation" (Sweet 1998).

There are many heroes between the lines in this story!

In prewar days, values were pretty basic and society in general was not as selfish and self-centered as the society we seem to live in today. We respected authority and believed in what our parents taught us. When Pearl Harbor was bombed on December 7, 1941, the country, with very minor exceptions, was unanimous in backing the decision to go to war. There was a unique togetherness in the country then, and it is hard to understand today's environment. There was a real belief in patriotism and the duty to serve your country. Most all of my peers enlisted voluntarily and went off to the unknown without any argument or excuses as to why they shouldn't.

It was a unique time in our history, and it was a unique group of young men who answered the call. Another factor, along with the men who brought about the success of the United States, of course, was the unbelievably rapid response and the overwhelming industrial strength brought to bear on the Axis powers (Germany, Italy, and Japan).

Above all, I truly believe that the patriotism of all Americans is an often-forgotten plus. We really believed we were doing the right thing. We came together as a people as never before.

ABOVE: *Two of the guys with a local buddy in the Philippines. (Source unknown)*

BELOW: *Five of the "men of war" of VPB-216 enjoying the sights and sounds of San Diego. Dick Agnello is second from the left. (Dick Agnello photo collection)*

56   *Seaplanes at War*

*Crew 6, VPB-28 preparing for a Black Cat night out of Jinamoc Island, in Leyte Gulf. (Frank L. Hannig photo collection)*

## CAMARADERIE

I think it has always been difficult, based on the many books I have read about World War II, for many people to understand the camaraderie and close friendships that developed during the war within any group that served together. In the Navy, it was especially evident in aircrews and submarine crews (as shown by the fact that these were volunteer jobs!).

The fascinating thing to me is that these relationships developed among people with whom one may have spent only ten to twelve months of life with. I sincerely believe that these friendships were built on the fact that our very lives depended upon others to do their jobs correctly. How we did our jobs often meant the difference between life and death.

There was an inherent discipline in aircrews, yet an informality too, between officers and enlisted personnel. This was quite different from shipboard relationships, where fraternization between officers and enlisted personnel was generally frowned upon. To a degree, this shipboard regimentation was due to the confines of living aboard ship month after month. Discipline there was seen as what made it all possible.

I am convinced, though, that the unique closeness in aircrew relationships sacrificed nothing in terms of discipline. In fact, I believe this camaraderie allowed for better discipline in the long run. It was based on respect for the individual, not just on the rank an individual held, where he fit in the Naval hierarchy.

I always attribute the closeness of aircrewmen to the amount of time we spent together flying or on buoy watch. And to the fact that aircrew personnel, along with submariners, were volunteers. They went into their jobs with a most positive attitude.

## SOMETHING SPECIAL

They came from everywhere, as Dick Gingrich said, rich men, poor men, teens and oldsters (in their twenties). Most had never flown before and knew only what they had read about airplanes. They were volunteers all; they wanted to fly!

For most, that was a good decision; for some it wasn't—but that's war. They had good training, which continued when they got their squadron assignments. The really proficient crews took advantage of cross-training opportunities, to prepare each crew member to do another man's job. If you couldn't cut it, you probably would soon be gone.

The fact that the Navy maintained continuity in crews was a big advantage in really building a team, not just a crew. They did this by relieving a crew, when it was time, as a crew, in almost all cases.

Aircrews were looked upon as something special. Those who didn't fly often had some amount of jealousy. Whether right or wrong, these bad feelings were seen by aircrewmen as just another piece of the morale puzzle. There was a certain glamor attached to flying in wartime, which was hard to fathom at times, especially when *that* guy on *that* ship or on *that* plane would really like to kill you before you kill him. War has no glamor except in Hollywood, where you can get shot at and still walk through an artillery barrage without getting an arm or a leg blown off—as opposed to real life, where, if you're shot down you stay down, or if you're captured, you might easily be decapitated by the enemy.

Aircrewmen were known as Airedales, and we got a fifty-percent increase in pay (officers *and* enlisted men) for our air hours. We had to log four hours' flight time a month to be eligible for these "flight skins."

There were special insignia for the enlisted crew members: aerial gunner, radar operator, then combat aircrew wings, with a provision for battle stars. The officers had their wings of gold, flight pay, and the nickname "brown shoes." (Shipboard officers wore black shoes.)

One indicator of the closeness of crew members is the fact that I don't ever remember a fight between members of our crew—and it was not uncommon for an enlisted member of a crew to "debate" with an officer or other crew member when he thought something was wrong or being done wrong. This was probably because each of us—machinists, radiomen, and

TOP: *VPB-20 crew ready for a Black Cat night out of Leyte Gulf. (Source unknown)*

MIDDLE: *VPB-216's Olympic ski team, 1944. (Dick Agnello photo collection)*

BOTTOM: *The last party for VPB-205 before heading west from Kaneohe, Hawaii. (Spud Pinkney photo collection)*

ABOVE: *VPB-28 shares a quiet cocktail hour after a difficult night for the skipper at the CPO Club. (Frank L. Hannig photo collection)*

BELOW: *A group of VPB-21ers the last night before leaving for Okinawa. Rodney Powers, crew 1, is third from left in the front row. (Jean Powers photo collection)*

ordnance men—knew that, due to enough cross-training, we all knew our jobs extremely well. So if one of us corrected another one, the correction was trusted as coming from someone who knew what he was talking about. Also, we socialized with many of our officers, which was highly unusual in the Navy, which was famous for having more of a caste system than the other services.

A big factor in the morale of aircrew, I think, was how proud we were of our responsibilities as aircrewmen. It may sound trite, but it made us different. To us, the enlisted crew, the combat aircrew wings we wore were sort of special.

## THE GLUE THAT HELD IT ALL TOGETHER

Here are some more words from my book, *The Sailor Aviators,* on aircrew camaraderie.

"Just as the family is the bellwether of society, the crew is the bellwether of a squadron. The longer a crew was together, the more efficient and effective it became. The discipline and direction became almost automatic. An individual seldom would even consider doing something wrong that might jeopardize the other members. 'What's best for the whole' was the underlying motto. The following comments bear real testimony to that. (Sweet 1998)"

ABOVE: *Hula dancers and cold beer on the way to the war. . . . Kaneohe, Bay, Oahu, Hawaii, July 1944. (B. J. Mountain photo collection)*

BELOW: *VPB-21 crewmen on Saipan: Christensen, Wall, Young, and "friend." (Art Kennedy photo collection)*

# THE MEN SPEAK

PILOT: The camaraderie and relationships of pilots and crews was extraordinary. The main thing that has stayed with me and impressed me over and over was the uniqueness of the relationship. Two of my crew, who were the best in their business, risked their lives several times for the safety of the plane and the crew.

PILOT: The little things, but very important at the time, made us like brothers. A lot of that feeling was also the hours we spent together because of buoy watch.

RADIOMAN: The camaraderie established during our relatively brief stay together was unbelievable. I had no contact with my crew from 1946 until 1992. The camaraderie was there after nearly a half a century. We hardly missed a beat in the BS.

I could go on and on with the same theme emerging. I do believe that the preponderance of reunions of World War II groups is proof positive of this camaraderie.

*Some of the overflow from the O Club on Mogmog. What's healthier than fresh air and Jim Beam on a tropical isle? (Art Kennedy photo collection)*

*Five of VPB-21's crew enjoying the stimulating environment of Mogmog Island and a few "premium" beers. (Bob Peyton photo collection)*

## A FITTING EPILOGUE

Dick Gingrich, in his epilogue for the book *Mariner/Marlin, Anywhere, Anytime*, put a nearly perfect perspective on why there is such camaraderie in a crew of a seaplane. It is quoted here:

> The Mariners and their offspring, the Marlin, meant more to their crews than just military equipment designed to further enforce national interests. Not only did these aircraft venture out alone through unfriendly skies for hours on end, with the nearest help hundreds of miles distant, but many long hours were spent aboard while secured to a sea buoy. For the crews sharing these experiences, bonds became established more than in perhaps any other military organization. (Mariner/Marlin Association 1993)

ABOVE: *Simms and Moriarty of VPB-21. "Let's step over to the Top of the Mark for a cool one—or the O Club at Tanapag!" (Art Kennedy photo collection)*

BELOW: *A group of "old salts" from VPB-21: ten of the original pilots. (Source unknown)*

# THE SQUADRONS

## VH AND VPB SQUADRON OVERVIEW

Each of the seaplane squadrons that served in the Pacific had a unique history. Many, many interesting stories are a legacy from their personnel. For this book I picked, for each squadron, short stores that highlight the accomplishments of that squadron. I sincerely hope that these selections reflect well on their squadrons and that I have not offended any person involved.

No story is meant to be unique to only "that" squadron. Rather, each story could have happened to any crew and represents in total a day in the life of an aircrew in a squadron fighting in the Pacific during World War II.

The squadrons that make up this story (which are listed in chapter two, in the section called "The Politics of War") were all posted to the Pacific theater of operations. To keep the length of this book manageable, I have used the central and western Pacific theaters to tell this story in the most understandable manner. The squadrons are all patrol bombing squadrons (VPBs) with the exception of the six air-sea rescue (VH) squadrons, often called Dumbos.

I like the Navy's separation of the Pacific Ocean into two theaters of operation, the central Pacific and the southwest Pacific. I do believe that prior to World War II, being of the

*Two Mariners on the field at Harvey Point, North Carolina, looking toward the Perquimans River. (Bill Ferrall photo collection)*

*Gassing up from a tanker truck on the ramp at Harvey Point, North Carolina. (Source unknown)*

*P-9 of VPB-202—the first squadron "over there"—resting at buoy in Tanapag, Saipan. (Doc Doherty photo collection)*

isolationist mind-set that most of us were, we did not consider that part of the world much more than an uncivilized, backward, and often barbaric part.

This concept of central and southwest Pacific seemed to be a natural for this story. From my limited viewpoint, the war was different in the two locales. For example, the Black Cat technique lent itself more to the southwest Pacific, with its innumerable harbors, inlets, rivers, and lagoons. The central Pacific was ideally suited to the PBM, with its long-range and staying power. There were planned missions that lasted up to thirteen hours or more.

Harvey Point, North Carolina, was the birthplace of most of the Pacific PBM squadrons; Charleston, South Carolina, and

Alameda, California, were the others. From those locations a squadron went on to NAS Kaneohe Bay, Oahu, Hawaii, and from there, on to combat.

The squadrons involved in the Pacific battleground were the fifteen patrol bombing squadrons (VPBs) and the six air-sea rescue (also known as Dumbo) squadrons (VHs). With a minor exception, all the aircraft were PBMs, the exception being that some VH squadrons also flew R4D-5s.

(Jim Sawruk of Allentown, Pennsylvania, a naval historian, has been most helpful as I have worked on this story. I have highlighted examples of his work that I found particularly interesting.)

## THE PIONEERS

VPB-202 and VPB-20 were pioneers for the rest of us. VPB-202 was the first PBM squadron to the Pacific, and it had knowledge to share with those who followed. VPB-20 was our first Black Cat squadron, and it too provided a good bit of new knowledge. As to the individual squadrons, a brief history follows for each, as well as some pertinent pictures.

*A VPB-20 PBM-3D cruising the Pacific for any likely target of opportunity. (Source unknown)*

## PATROL BOMBING SQUADRON 16 (VPB-16).

Established at NAS Norfolk, Virginia, in late 1943, the commanding officer was William J. Scarpino. Early in January 1944 the squadron moved to Naval Auxiliary Air Station (NAAS) Harvey Point, North Carolina, about sixty miles south of Norfolk, where shakedown training took place. Upon completion of training, they deployed to NAS Kaneohe Bay, Hawaii.

The road to Kaneohe was fraught with problems. First, one of the planes en route to NAS Alameda, California, crashed in the desert between Eagle Mountain Lake, Texas, and San Diego with the loss of the whole crew. It was determined that there was instant engine failure! There were two other engine problems, with both planes lost. The crews were saved, however. This series of accidents started a rumor that there was some sabotage involved, but the rumor was never proven.

It wasn't over yet. Once more plane had to make an emergency landing near Howland Island, of Amelia Earhart fame. The landing was rough, but the crew got out and made it ashore in the life rafts. The island was deserted, fortunately, as it was still in Japanese control, and the crew was picked up the following day. This was the only island in World War II captured by a PBM!

When all planes reached Eniwetok, they were assigned patrols throughout the Marshall Islands until June 14, 1944. Then six of the crews left for Saipan, where the invasion was under way. They flew from a seadrome that was set up four miles offshore, in the open sea.

The arrival of VPB-16 at Saipan coincided with the first long-range patrols. Their activities were soon supplemented by the arrival of VPB-202 and -216. The patrols flown by these squadrons were instrumental in setting up the famous Marianas turkey shoot. This was a most significant battle between major carrier forces of the United States and Japan. It resulted in, for all practical purposes, the beginning of the demise of the Japanese Naval Air Force as a really effective weapon. The score of this now-famous air battle was 294 Japanese planes lost to 31 United States downed planes! Not that the Japanese didn't continue to fly and fight, but the best of their carrier pilots were becoming pretty well thinned out. VPB-16's patrols were also instrumental in the initiation of the battles of the Philippine Sea. These two battles on June 19 and 20 resulted in Japan's losing 476 planes and 450 aviators.

On June 20, one of VPB-16's Mariners was shot down by friendly fire, killing the whole crew. Shortly thereafter, a P-61 Black Widow fighter shot down another of VPB-16's Mariners as it was taking off from Tanapag seaplane base. There were no casualties this time, though, and the plane was salvaged.

In September 1944 VPB-16 was ordered to the Palau Islands, specifically Kossol Passage, another open sea seadrome and what would turn out to be a very difficult operating area. VPB-216, -17, -21, and -202 also went. From Kossol Passage, missions were flown as far as Samar in the Philippines, to support of one of the greatest sea battles in history, the battle of the Philippine Sea in Leyte Gulf.

**PATROL BOMBING SQUADRON 17 (VPB-17)** was established at NAS Norfolk, Virginia, on January 3, 1944. The commanding officer was Lcdr. Kenneth A. Kuehner. The squadron moved to Harvey Point NAAS, and deployed to Kaneohe, Hawaii, on April 17, 1944. After further training and flying some operational patrols, the squadron left for Kwajalein on September 1, and then on to the southwest Pacific. Action picked up dramatically and was recorded by the war correspondent, Merrill Mueller:

One of VPB-17's planes was shot down by a Japanese

*Box 10, the "Mighty Ten-der" of VPB-17, on the way to Saipan on Christmas Day 1944. In the waist hatch is Vance Kyle, ARM. (Vance Kyle photo collection)*

destroyer off the China coast. Ltjg. Fred Forman, PPC (patrol plane commander) was knocked unconscious when the plane exploded and crashed. Ensign Bob Bunge, who also survived, found an inflated life raft and got Forman into it. For four long days and nights, with little water and no food, they drifted. Finally, on the fifth day, they saw land. Shortly afterward, a junk appeared with eight men aboard. They picked the two men up. After a long and arduous journey over land, using every means of transport—rickshaw, horseback, etc.—they made it to safety. Although they had become separated, they made their ways individually to safety and celebrated their good luck together!

And a second story, as told in this telex:

> LT. WARREN LASSER OF WATERLOO, IOWA, 28-YEAR-OLD SKIPPER OF THE PLANE, DROPPED THE BOMBS WHILE HIS CREW MANNED THEIR POSTS AND DID THE GUNNING OF A CONVOY OF FIVE SHIPS.
>
> THIS WAS THE FIRST REAL BLACK CAT ATTACK BY CREW 10 OF VPB-17 ON A ROUTINE MISSION. THIS WAS AN EXTRAORDINARY MISSION, AS NO OTHER SQUADRON HAD A SINGLE PLANE ATTACK AND SINK A WHOLE CONVOY OF JAPANESE SHIPS . . . FIVE SHIPS, TOTALING 17,000 TONS.
>
> THIS IS MERRILL MUELLER REPORTING FROM MANILA.

*A bunch of the big birds on the water at Kerama-retto, with a VPB-17 Black Cat in the foreground. (John Hook photo collection)*

*Plane 13 (Bu. No. 45368) of VPB-17 tied up at buoy with its PPC in the cockpit, Saipan, October 1944. (L. H. Roberts photo collection)*

Eventually, the squadron ended up at Tawitawi flying ASW patrols. Then an unusual opportunity arose—the chance to fly for the allied intelligence bureau. These flights carried supplies and personnel from Morotai to guerilla groups on the coast of North Borneo. A Captain Chipper of the Australian army flew with the crew and was an excellent source of information about Semporna, Labuan Island, and Maradu Bay. As the war began to wind down, VPB-17 was instrumental in getting some POWs out who had been captives of the Japanese in North Borneo.

## PATROL BOMBING SQUADRON 18 (VPB-18) was established at NAS Norfolk, Virginia, and moved to Charleston, South Carolina, for shakedown, and then to Kaneohe, Hawaii; Lcdr. C. R. Brower commanding.

Here is some information about aerial battles between PBMs and Japanese aircraft. VPB-18 had an excellent record in aerial battles, as attested to by Jim Sawruk's research.

*April 16, 1945:* Two PBMs from VPB-18, flown by Jordan Collins and Paul Fitzgerald, shot down a Japanese E13A (Jake). This Jake was from the 901 Ku Hakata detachment and was

*A VPB-18 Mariner shot down by a Japanese fighter. The other plane's float, left center of photo, indicates that the crew is about to be rescued.. (Bill Ferrall photo collection)*

*Harvey Herzog, VPB-18, playing pilot, but he was really "doing windows." (VPB-18 photo collection)*

commanded by Ensign Yoichiro Shiobara. The Jake's crew of three was lost in this flight.

*May 15, 1945:* Two PBMs from VPB-18 again engaged Japanese aircraft from the 343 Ku Fighter Kikotai 701. The VPB-18 aircraft were on an antishipping strike in the Tsushima Straits. They sank one ship along their return track. Four fighters took off after the two PBMs initially, with four more to follow. However, two of the later group missed forming up, and another from the later group had engine trouble and had to return. As such, five Japanese fighters attacked the PBMs multiple times.

The PBMs were commanded by Ltjg. I. E. Marr and Lt. M. E. Hart. It was Hart's first patrol and Lt. E. C. Dixon was aboard, acting as checkout pilot for him. In a short but vicious fight, both PBMs were shot down. Marr and his entire crew were lost. Before they went down, however, they did shoot down one Japanese aircraft, whose pilot was also lost.

In total, the PBMs claimed two Zekes, one Tony, and one Tojo. It is now known that all of the aircraft engaged were N1K (Georges) flown by Ltjg. Akio Matsuba (wounded in action), CPO Takumi Sagitaki, CPO Takeo Yamada, PO1 Nobuyori Minoura (killed in action), CPO Takamiki Kashima. One George was lost outright, while two more crash landed after being hit. (Courtesy of Jim Sawruk)

Note that the Japanese had enlisted mates as pilots throughout the war. Our naval aviation pilots (enlisted)—NAPs—were phased out by 1942.

VPB-18 had an outstanding record: 12 planes shot down, 34 ships sunk, and many more aggressive attacks on enemy installations and equipment.

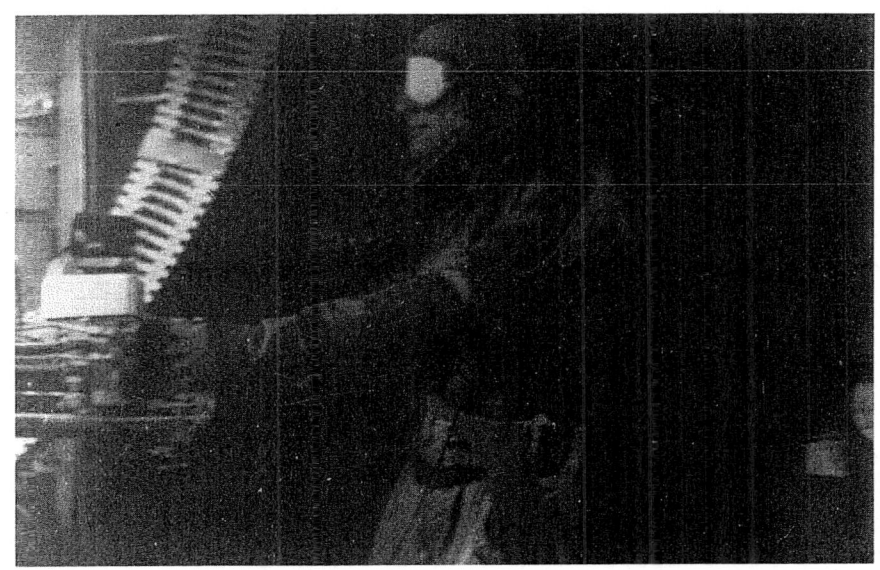

*Harvey Herzog of VPB-18 pours it on to a small Japanese ship in the South China Sea. See also next photo. (Source unknown)*

*A small Japanese ship in the South China Sea is attacked by VPB-18. See also previous photo. (Source unknown)*

*Pretty good tally sheet—about the best in the Pacific Mariner community. (Mariner/Marlin Newsletter photo collection)*

**PATROL BOMBING SQUADRON 19 (VPB-19)** was established, and trained at NAS Alameda, California, one of several PBM squadrons that trained on the West Coast. The best-known story about VPB-19 is as follows:

> When a plane was being ferried west for VPB-19 it ran into trouble. Forced into a single-engine operation, the crew made a successful landing in the desert, on Willcox dry lake, fortunately sustaining very little damage.
>
> Mechanics were flown to the site to check out the engines. They gave the plane a thorough check and cleared it to fly. A set of modified beaching gear was sent to the site. The plan was to attempt takeoff, then drop the wheels into the desert once they got airborne. This plan was jokingly designated as "the one and only PBM-3DA."
>
> After a surprisingly trouble-free takeoff, the plane flew to NAS Alameda, where it made a satisfactory landing. It was later christened *The Miracle of Willcox Dry Lake* and rejoined the Navy's operational seaplanes.

*The USS* Hamlin *at Iwo Jima on a relatively calm day. Note how the port float of VPB-19's Mariner is cutting through the peaceful sea. (George Lindberg photo collection)*

A great Dumbo story takes place near Ponape, one of the increasing number of islands bypassed by U.S. ground troops. A Marine pilot had been shot down while making a bombing run on Ponape. His Corsair fighter was hit by antiaircraft fire and he made a successful landing in a rough sea, in thirty-foot swells. Then a Mariner piloted by Navy Lt. C. M. Rees dropped a six-man raft, which allowed the Marine to exit his one-man raft, which was being tossed around like a matchstick. Once in the new raft, the Marine started to drift toward the Japanese-occupied island.

Rees saw the raft heading for the shore, so, with a quick vote of his crew, he decided to attempt a landing. Pretty sure he wouldn't be able to take off again, he made a nice landing —within pistol range of the Japanese—and rescued the downed Marine. "I didn't see how he could make it with the sea running the way it was, but he did," the Marine later said. Takeoff, as predicted, was impossible. Taxiing was the only answer, and taxi they did—for fourteen hours, all through the night, in a tropical storm, with their radio out of commission. A horrible night, but prayers were answered when at dawn a destroyer escort arrived on the scene and took all of the survivors aboard.

(The sequel to this story: After taxiing all night, the destroyer escort that picked up the survivors collided with the PBM and tore the wingtip and pontoon off one wing. As the plane rolled over, all of the survivors abandoned ship, and made it onto the DE and up the cargo nets to safety.)

In September 1944 VPB-19 made a major contribution to the seaplane war. Under the command of Lcdr. J. A. Masterson, the squadron completed the testing of the newly developed device, JATO (pronounced *jay-toe*).

*Crew 14 of VPB-19 takes it slow and easy! (Source unknown)*

The Men and Their Squadrons

*A well-prepared buoy watch on a VPB-19 Mariner at Iwo Jima. (Source unknown)*

JATO, the jet-assisted takeoff device, was a jet-powered unit that attached to the fuselage of the plane. With this additional power—some four thousand pounds of thrust—the plane could take off in half the space required without JATO. Initial statistics listed planes getting airborne in eight to ten seconds as opposed to the fifty to seventy seconds for the PBMs without JATO. JATO was a real boost (no pun intended) to open-sea operations.

There was not even the semblance of a harbor or protected area at Iwo Jima, so a whole new set of tactics was necessary to cope with Iwo's seas. There were lots of problems to cope with, like bodies, cartons, ammo boxes—all the debris of war in the water. This often caused the planes to taxi three to five miles out in order to take off. The sea and the weather took a real toll on the planes and ended up negating the use of PBMs from Iwo. Fortunately the island had an airstrip that was secured a few days prior to the surrender of the island. Then land-based patrol planes could be utilized.

(JATO was a godsend that allowed takeoffs to be as short as eight to ten seconds— invaluable in the open sea. Takeoffs without JATO, as lots of us know, could last for a minute and ten seconds . . . which doesn't sound like much, but when you're bouncing around inside the plane it often seems like a lifetime.)

### PATROL BOMBING SQUADRON 20 (VPB-20)

was established in February 1944 at NAS Alameda, California. June first saw the squadron deployed to Kaneohe Bay, Hawaii. Finally, in October, they moved to the seaplane base at Manus in the

Admiralties, now part of Papua New Guinea. VPB-20 was the first PBM squadron to go to the southwest Pacific. Once in Manus, their PBMs were painted black and nicknamed "Black Cats," after the PBYs that had been flying night flights in the Pacific since 1942.

Exhaust-stack suppressers were also installed, which made the plane almost totally invisible at night by hiding its exhaust flames. These night flights were flown at very low altitudes and were long ones. The average flight for VPB-20's Black Cats was thirteen hours; their longest logged flight was fourteen and a half hours.

VPB-20 gets my personal vote for being one of the most successful squadrons that fought in the Pacific. Recognizing the occasional folly of statistics, one must still start somewhere, so here goes. VPB-20, flying many Black Cat missions, shot down 2 enemy planes and damaged 9. They sank 44 ships, with another 32 damaged (approximately 130,000 tons). They rescued 24 aviators and bombed 24 land installations. Their flying time exceeded 5,000 hours: flying 236 days, 159 nights, and 27 special missions. The squadron earned many commendations and medals.

One of the PBM operational manuals spelled out the Black Cat technique:

> The doctrine set for Black Cat missions was "plenty rugged," being dusk-to-dawn flights. The first consideration after takeoff was gasoline. It was necessary to conserve in every possible way. Low-power settings were used whenever possible.
>
> The only difference between the attack run and normal cruise was that the engines were put into auto-rich when in range of enemy fire. The flight to the target area was

*The enlisted contingent of VPB-20 posing in their dress blues—not a dirty hat in the crowd! (B. Carl Horton photo collection)*

maintained at two hundred fifty feet or less, and once over the target area, the altitude, many times, was lowered to absolute minimum in order to effect undetected attacks on enemy strongholds.

Radar served as the eyes of the plane, guiding it between and over the numerous protruding rocks and islands that lined the coast. Entries into bays and rivers were made by radar. The attack run was guided by radar, as the target often remained invisible until illuminated by the plane's .50-caliber tracer bullets.

Radar operators, whether they were ordnancemen, aviation mechanics, or radiomen, were soon able to distinguish between rocks, junks, and prospective targets. No matter how proficient the radar operator or how good the radar, there was no substitute for contact flights under a full moon (called a "bomber's moon"). Flights were completed in darkness, in fog, or in moonlight. It was not the policy to cancel flights or to return to base because of weather. Fronts were usually entered without a change of heading, but at low altitude to avoid turbulence.

[Addendum to the PBM operations manual for the southwestern Pacific:] *If shot down, paint your ass green and head for the hills!*

Flying the Black Cat missions put crews under tremendous, stress, as one can imagine. An interesting story is the following.

On the night of November 27–28, 1944, one Black Cat PBM commanded by Ltjg. John B. Mouio was providing air coverage for four of our destroyers (DESDIV-43), which were bombarding Japanese positions in the Ormoc Bay area of the Philippines. The PBM made radar contact north of Ponson

*Officers of VPB-20 in their dress blues—pretty spiffy-looking group! (B. Carl Horton photo collection)*

Island. Investigating, Mouio sighted a submarine moving east into Ormoc Bay.

The sighting was reported to the destroyers, who quickly made contact and illuminated the target at 0132 on the morning of November 28. At 0135 they opened fire, and by 0145 the submarine was seen sinking by the stem.

The destroyers involved were the *Waller* (DD-466), *Saufley* (DD-465), *Renshaw* (DD-499), and *Pringle* (DD-477).

For many years it has been speculated that the sub was the I-41 or I-46, but nobody knew for sure. Recent information has verified this sinking to be the Japanese army transport submarine *Yu2*.

ABOVE: *A VPB-20 Black Cat being lifted aboard the USS* Tangier *for engine work. (Source unknown)*

BELOW: *A VPB-20 Black Cat coming on board the USS* Tangier, *somewhere in the southwest Pacific, for engine change. (Bill Ferrall photo collection)*

**PATROL BOMBING SQUADRON 21 (VPB-21)** was established at NAS Norfolk on March 23, 1944, and moved to Harvey Point, North Carolina, the next day under the command of Lcdr. James Daugherty. They left for the West Coast (Alameda) on June 17, and a few days later were off to the war via Kaneohe Bay, Hawaii. One of the more interesting incidents VPB-21 was involved in is below.

On April 7, 1945 the Japanese decided to attack Okinawa with a fleet spearheaded by the *Yamato*, the world's biggest battleship. The task force was to cause maximum damage on the landing force on the island. The task force consisted of the *Yamato*, one Agano-class fighter cruiser—the *Yahagi*—and eight destroyers. As was learned later, the Japanese had fuel enough for only a one-way trip, so this was truly a suicide attack. This was part of a planned *kikusui* attack that included 355 kamikaze planes and the same number of conventional planes attacking Okinawa. (A *kikusui* was a massive kamikaze attack, used toward the end of the war to defend the Japanese homeland. The word literally means "floating chrysanthemum," and they needed to be seen to be believed. There were ten *kikusui* attacks, dating from April 6, 1945, through June 22, 1945.)

The plan for the *Yamato* was to fight through to the beach at Okinawa, ground the ship and go to work destroying as much as possible of the occupying force with the ship's eighteen-inch guns. These guns could hurl a shell weighing more than a ton some thirty-five miles.

The Japanese task force sailed out of the inland sea and south toward Okinawa. Fortunately, two U.S. submarines saw

*On the way to war, smiling and alive. Original personnel of VPB-21, June 1944, at NAS Kaneohe, Hawaii. (Source unknown)*

*Crew 14 of VPB-21 posing by Bu. No. 45362,* Charlot the Harlot. *The first* Charlot *was lost at Palau. (Don Sweet photo collection)*

them and identified the individual ships. Then at 0957 on April 7, Dick Simms of VPB-21, along with Jim Young, also of VPB-21, made visual contact.

For the next two hours, the two Mariners shadowed the task force under a hail of antiaircraft [the *Yamato* alone had 146 antiaircraft guns]. Young and Simms and crews helped coordinate the attacks of all the U.S. carrier planes that had arrived from Task Force 58.

The Japanese task force was decimated by the U.S. carrier aircraft. The *Yamato* sank with 2,400 sailors on board. It was learned later that of the 2,650-man crew, only some 250 survived! Another 800 to 1,000 Japanese sailors died when their cruiser and two destroyers were also sunk. Two other destroyers were damaged enough so that they later had to be scuttled. The remaining four destroyers escaped.

Meanwhile, Jim Young made an open-sea landing to pick up a lone American aviator in a life raft. This was completed successfully in spite of continual enemy fire. Young landed, picked up the downed pilot, Ltjg. Delaney, and made a beautiful JATO takeoff with Delaney, who had dropped four 500-pound bombs on the *Yamato* and was the only survivor of his TBM torpedo bomber. Delaney was unhurt, and they made it safely back to base.

80  Seaplanes at War

# PATROL BOMBING SQUADRON 22 (VPB-22) was established at NAAS Harvey Point, North Carolina, and took the regular route to the war.

If there is any doubt about flying from Kossol Passage in the Palau Islands, I think these entries from Bob Willig's (a radioman in VPB-22) diary should certainly dispel a lot of misunderstanding. The Passage was truly open sea, and it tested both the aircrews and the tough old Mariners to their utmost.

> *Nov. 20, 1944:* Will be here at Kossol Passage for six to eight weeks. Japs on island only eight miles away. Approximately 40,000 of them. Planes and tender USS *Casco* anchored eight miles offshore. F4U Corsairs strafed island yesterday. Expect big storm. If it comes any closer we will fly over to New Guinea this afternoon.

> *Nov. 29, 1944:* After flying patrol all night, we landed at 0600. Just finished eating morning chow and all crews were called to their planes to take off at once. The Japs are headed for our ships with thirty Bettys [medium bombers]; it's a suicide squadron coming to bomb us. The Japs arrived, but the only one that got through the fighters caused no real damage.

OPPOSITE PAGE, TOP: *The* Yamato, *the world's biggest battleship at the time, under way on a suicide run on Okinawa, while Okinawa was being invaded by U.S. forces. The other ships are cruisers and destroyers. For more of this story, see text on VPB-21.* (VPB-21 Crews 6 and 8 photo collection)

OPPOSITE PAGE, BOTTOM: *The* Yamato *on fire and sinking after being attacked by scores of carrier planes after being tracked by Simms and Young from VPB-21. They directed the carrier planes' attack while ducking antiaircraft fire from the* Yamato. (VPB-21 Crews 6 and 8 photo collection)

BELOW: *Dick Simms and John Hook fighting off five Japanese fighters (Georges).* (USS Chandeleur photo collection)

Seaplanes at War

OPPOSITE, TOP: *A Japanese fighter drops a phosphorus bomb near V-10—no damage, no casualties.* (USS Chandeleur *photo collection*)

OPPOSITE, BOTTOM: *A Japanese fighter makes a pass at Simms's plane.* (USS Chandeleur *photo collection*)

BELOW: *Simms trying to evade a Japanese fighter—too late. Simms was badly shot up and eventually went down. All this took place just off the coast of Japan.* (USS Chandeleur *photo collection*)

84   Seaplanes at War

OPPOSITE, TOP: *Six of V-10's crew in rafts!* (USS Chandeleur *photo collection*)

OPPOSITE, BOTTOM: *Four of Simms's crew and the chief aerographer from the* Chandeleur *awaiting pickup by a Dumbo plane from VH-3.* (USS Chandeleur *photo collection*)

LEFT: *Ernie Delaney, pilot of a TBM that dropped four bombs on the* Yamato, *was shot down, then rescued by Jim Young and a crew of VPB-21.* (Source unknown)

NEXT PAGE: *"How sweet it is." Crew V-8 getting on board VH-3's Mariner after a night afloat off the Japanese coast.* (USS Chandeleur *photo collection*)

*Dec. 12, 1944:* Plane 13, with crew 2 flying it, *crashed* on takeoff this morning; plane damaged beyond repair. It was quickly pulled aboard tender and stripped. Failed to mention, plane 5 was badly damaged when it made a *crash landing* at sea after one engine failed about two weeks ago, while on night patrol.

*Dec. 14, 1944:* Plane 14 *crashed* last night when landing. They had gotten lost in the typhoon and were three hours overdue. They came in at 2030. While landing, depth charges dropped from bomb bays and exploded. The entire tail was blown off and the hull was ripped open. The plane sank in fifteen minutes, but all hands were saved.

**PATROL BOMBING SQUADRON 25 (VPB-25)** was established as Patrol Squadron 25 on April 28, 1944, under the command of Lcdr. James C. Skorcz. On August 21, 1944, the squadron began their move west. After their move to Kaneohe Bay, Oahu, Hawaii, and further training, they deployed to the Philippines, San Pedro Bay, Leyte Gulf, in November 1944.

There was lots of inhuman behavior during World War II, as in all wars. The Japanese were particularly sadistic, as shown in the following story.

VPB-25 was operating in the southwest Pacific area. On June 24, 1945, Lt. D. J. Croze and his crew were patrolling off the east coast of Borneo and eventually ran across two Sugar Dogs [small Japanese freighters] with a sub chaser as an escort.

ABOVE: *Six guys on the tail. "It's a big plane, isn't it?"* (Vince Walka photo collection)

FACING PAGE: *"How sweet it is."* Crew V-8 getting on board VH-3's Mariner after a night afloat off the Japanese coast. (USS Chandeleur photo collection)

LEFT: *VPB-22, crew 11, 1944–45,* Front row, left to right: Louis Fusco, radio; Lloyd Thompson, ordnance; Bob Willig, flight engineer; Rosie Cannizzaro, flight engineer; Tom Murray, radio; Bill Waldon, flight engineer; Omer Carrico, ordnance. Back row left to right: Wayne Tadman, crew chief; Ens. L. Strawser; Lt. H. Strohoefer; Ens. C. Lamb; John McMullen, radio. (Source unknown)

*The Men and Their Squadrons*

Croze immediately mounted an attack on the three ships. The sub-chaser gun crew were pumping out heavy antiaircraft fire, but Croze had hits on both Sugar Dogs, and one immediately sank. The antiaircraft fire was being delivered very accurately from the sub chaser, and the Mariner was hit twice in its gas tanks, causing two men to be wounded and one to later lose his foot. Croze knew he could not make it back to base, so he landed at Lingayen Island, just off of the Japanese-held Celebes. He went ashore but learned nothing, so he gave up for the night.

In the morning, one of the radiomen tried to make contact with base, but the Japanese saw him and he was killed. That precipitated an every-man-for-himself movement, and the rest of the crew—nine men—scattered. Three members hid in the water for three days, but the sharks found them and attacked, mangling the left arm of one of them, Dale Huntone. Fortunately for them, just after the attack a Mariner from VPB-21 picked up the three survivors from the water and one from the brush. Huntone lost his arm in short order. Four crew members were never seen again. After the war was over, however, it was proven that all four of them were captured and beheaded.

## PATROL BOMBING SQUADRON 26 (VPB-26)

went through training procedures with no real problems. They arrived on Okinawa in April 1945. From there they had the singular honor of being the first seaplane squadron to bomb any target on the Japanese homeland. There were so many targets of opportunity along the coast of the island of Shikoku, and the pilots of VPB-26 had been eager to go after some of them. Their opportunity came on June 15, and its success is related below.

On June 15, 1945, two of VPB-26's Mariners attacked a shipyard on Shikoku, taking the enemy completely by surprise [those of you who know can't imagine the venerable, gull-winged PBM surprising anyone!]. They left one ship sinking

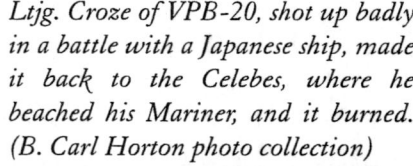

*Ltjg. Croze of VPB-20, shot up badly in a battle with a Japanese ship, made it back to the Celebes, where he beached his Mariner, and it burned. (B. Carl Horton photo collection)*

*Jinamoc Island, Philippines. VPB-25 in January 1945. Pappy Custon is fifth from the right. (Source unknown)*

and a shipyard in flames. Continuing on their patrol, they found many more targets as they turned for home, including a number of ships, a passenger ferry, a radio station near the harbor, and another, smaller shipyard, which they left in flames. Antiaircraft fire was getting heavy and more accurate, so it seemed that discretion was the better part of valor. They hightailed it out of there.

Two days later, on June 17, two more of VPB-26's Mariners attacked a shipyard and adjoining railyards in the harbor area of Susaki. Damage was quite extensive. The shipyard was left in ruins, a number of railroad cars were destroyed, six Sugar Dogs were destroyed, a ferry boat was damaged and beached, and eleven more Sugar Dogs were destroyed, a ferry boat was strafed and badly damaged and forced aground. Twelve new Sugar Dogs were strafed and left afire. Quite a two-day record!

Then another first for VPB-26: it had the first Navy seaplane to land in Tokyo Bay, and was the first squadron to operate there. The date was August 8, 1945.

## PATROL BOMBING SQUADRON 27 (VPB-27).

The written history of VPB-27 begins:

> *Down where the Perquimans River drains lazily out of the Great Dismal Swamp into Albemarle Sound, a momentous ceremony occurred the afternoon of June 1, 1944. That is, it was a momentous event for the two hundred twenty-five officers and men who were to comprise the complement of Patrol Bombing Squadron 27.*

The following is a story from that squadron.

On August 7, 1945, at 1800 hours, two of VPB-27's Mariners left the Kerama-retto seadrome and headed for their planned antishipping sweep off Formosa. About two hours later they were strafing some enemy PT boats. Their heavy fire drove the heavily damaged PTs (three of them) onto the beach. VPB-27 then radioed base and informed them of the action. . . . That was the last word heard from the planes. Searches for the two planes continued for several days, but to no avail.

Some eleven days later, at VPB-27's base was notified that the only trace of the two planes was a wingtip floating in the general vicinity of where the planes had last been seen. This was the only clue ever found, so both planes with their crews were marked off as missing in action and presumed lost.

TOP: *VPB-27 Mariner takes off from Oahu, Hawaii, after some R&R — with designated driver.* (Bill Ferrall photo collection)

BOTTOM: *VPB-27, crew 2's E2, Dinah Might . . . She did!* (Bill Ferrall photo collection)

# PATROL BOMBING SQUADRON 28 (VPB-28).

On July 28, 1944, VPB-28 was established at Harvey Point, North Carolina, under CO John L. Elwell. This was the last PBM squadron to be formed in World War II. By January 1945 they were operating in two areas, one detachment from Mindoro and the other from Lingayen Gulf. Patrols were flown in the Indo-China and Hainan Island areas. For several months they flew Black Cat missions, with great success.

On April 1st, D-day at Okinawa, one of VPB-28's Mariners was patrolling between the Pescadores [islands west of Formosa] and Tainan and made contact with a destroyer escort. An immediate attack was mounted. Two bombing runs

TOP: *VPB-27's crew 2. Bill Ferrall—without whom this book would not exist!—is in the front row, far right. (Bill Ferrall photo collection)*

BOTTOM: *Five of the stalwarts from VPB-27. Left to right. Gene Cheak, Bill Ferrall, Sam Whitmore, Earl Corbin, Ken Woodruff. Discussing "strategy for Okinawa." (Bill Ferrall photo collection)*

*The Men and Their Squadrons*

resulted in one hit amidships with a 500-pound bomb, a near miss at the stern with a 250-pound bomb, and then another 500-pounder that lifted the bow out of the water and left it motionless. It was determined that it probably sank later. This was just one of some 77,000 tons of shipping attacked between March 1, 1945, and April 23, 1945, with excellent results.

Admiral Kincaid commended VPB-28 on their many achievements against Japanese shipping:

> *It is with the greatest satisfaction that I forward the following message from Commander Seventh Fleet: "Congratulations on the record you have achieved in the last three months. You have hit the enemy many times where it hurts the most. Your perseverance and devotion to duty reflect the highest credit on VPB-28 and the pilots and aircrewmen who participated in these actions."*

*VPB-28's plane 108, a Black Cat, at the buoy at Tawitawi, Philippines. (Bob Van Trieste photo collection)*

*The VPB-28 ready room on Jinamoc Island, Leyte Gulf, the Philippines. Briefing a couple of crews for a Black Cat night. (Frank L. Hannig photo collection)*

## PATROL BOMBING SQUADRON 202 (VPB-202)

had been established at the Naval Air Station at Corpus Christi, Texas, in late 1942. The commanding officer was Lcdr. C. C. McCauley. From Corpus Christi, the squadron transferred to Key West, Florida, on February 5, 1943. They trained at that base and then deployed to a forward base at Grand Cayman to search for subs in the Gulf. Back to Key West NAS, to be outfitted with PBM-3Ds, then deployed to the Pacific theater. They moved to San Diego NAS in mid-December 1943, where there was a change of command. Commander Robert W. Leeman took charge. From that time forward VPB-202 was known as "Leeman's Demons."

*D-2 VPB-28, forced down by engine trouble between Leyte and Samar, is being towed into Leyte by the crash boat seen above. (Source unknown)*

*The VPB-28 skipper and some of the boys have a drink after a long day at the office. (Frank L. Hannig photo collection)*

On December 16, 1944, they moved to NAS Kaneohe, Hawaii, and then on to Tarawa in the Gilbert Islands, and began patrol duty as the first PBM squadron in the Pacific.

In January 1944 Lt. Hunt of VPB-202 made the first bombing raid on Japanese positions (by a Martin Mariner). It was a relatively successful raid with damage to the runway and surrounding installations on Taroa Island in the Marshall Islands chain.

They then deployed to Majuro and flew patrols from there with occasional bombing attacks on Ponape. Finally, they were relieved and returned to Kaneohe for some maintenance and R&R. On the sixteenth of April the squadron was again to be a "first" as they headed back to the war. This time to be part of the Saipan invasion and then on to Palau. By November they were on their way home to the States, having set the stage for the rest of us, who learned from their activities and tactics.

They were truly pioneers and we all followed their lead.

### PATROL BOMBING SQUADRON 205 (VPB-205).

Patrol Bombing Squadron VPB-205 reported to Fleet Air Wing Five, Naval Auxiliary Air Station, Harvey Point, North Carolina, in January 1944, commanded by Lcdr. H. E. Hanset, just recently returned from duty in Trinidad and Puerto Rico, in the West Indies. After completing shakedown they made the trip west and boarded their tender, the USS *St. George*, AV-16, that had been damaged in a kamikaze attack at Okinawa and had retired for repairs. It was now ready for redeployment to Okinawa.

While stationed at Okinawa, after the war ended in August, one of the VPB-205 Mariners was on patrol and dis-

*The USS* Curtiss *at Kerama-retto. A PBM is on the seaplane deck, and a Grumman Duck on the extreme port side of the seaplane deck. (Bill Ferrall photo collection)*

appeared. The squadron mounted a search, but unfortunately they never found a trace of the plane. The search resumed later in September, but again no luck. It was assumed it would never be found.

But many years later Spud Pinkney, a pilot in VPB-205, heard what happened. The Japanese, as another antiaircraft weapon, had installed heavy steel cables to the tops of mountains, stretching them across so that they would interfere with low-flying planes. The story was that the VPB-205 plane had hit one of the cables and crashed, and was scattered over several mountains. Another unusual story from World War II!

## PATROL BOMBING SQUADRON 208 (VPB-208).

On December 15, 1942, at NAS Norfolk, Virginia, Patrol Squadron 208 (VPB-208) was established. Lcdr. David Goodman was commanding officer, and Lt. R. Leeman executive officer.

On January 1, 1943, training started at Corpus Christi, Texas. From there they went to NAS Key West, Florida. Finally they moved to Harvey Point NAAS, and then on to NAS Kaneohe Bay, Hawaii. At Kaneohe they finished operational training and moved on to Kerama-retto.

On the night of April 27–28, 1944, three VPB-208 planes were launched just before dark to participate with three VPB-27 planes in a night attack on an enemy convoy in the East China Sea.

Since seaplanes were the only aircraft in the area with the range to do the job, these two squadrons were chosen. They would fly to within fifty miles of the convoy and then drop to an altitude of fifty feet to make their bombing run.

When they were twenty-five miles out, the convoy started putting up antiaircraft fire. The tracers and antiaircraft bursts surpassed any Fourth of July fireworks display the aircrews had ever seen. The Mariners made the attack through a veritable hail of enemy light-, medium-, and heavy-duty antiaircraft fire. All the Mariners were badly shot up. Several men suffered minor wounds, but no one was killed. Severe damage was inflicted on at least two enemy ships.

Upon arriving back at base, the Mariners had to circle for quite some time, as a Japanese air raid was in progress. The landing was anything but routine, since there were no runway lights, no landing lights, and the aileron cables on one of 208's planes were broken.

The month of April proved to be a busy one for VPB-208. They flew more hours than any of the other squadrons operating out of Kerama-retto. In early May the squadron shot down four

BELOW AND ON FACING PAGE: *VPB-208's D-15 in big trouble—a losing battle at Kerama-retto with rough waters.* (USS Hamlin *photo collection*)

enemy planes and damaged three others in air battles. On June 6, five more enemy planes were shot up badly. Also, in early May and June four enemy ships were sunk and seven were damaged. In July, two ships were sunk and seven were damaged.

**PATROL BOMBING SQUADRON 216 (VPB-216)** was established in December 1943 and reported to Harvey Point, North Carolina, for shakedown. With training completed, they left for the West Coast, went on to Kaneohe, Hawaii, and then to the war on March 24, 1944. The CO was Harry E. Cook Jr. After arriving at Saipan the squadron began flying missions such as the ones described below.

VPB-216 had one of the first aerial battles of a Mariner against a Japan plane. This battle was between a VPB-216 Mari-

*(See facing page for caption.)*

*Two of VPB-208's PBM-3Ds cruising and looking for someone to give a bruisin' to. (Bill Ferrall photo collection)*

ner and a Japanese Emily, an H8K flying boat, which was widely acknowledged to be the best flying boat of World War II.

> H. H. Crum Jr., a patrol plane commander in VPB-216, ran across the Emily while on patrol out of Saipan. This contact initiated a running forty-five-minute gun battle. The Emily was more heavily gunned (carrying 20-millimeter guns) and Crum did a good job of maneuvering the Mariner, knowing he was outgunned. He chased the Emily, smoking heavily, in the direction of its home base.

There was no known conclusion, but it was certainly a moral victory and most likely an air victory.

There are many strange stories and any of us who were downed in the water had to have some concerns. I think most people can't imagine anything much worse than being eaten alive:

> In October 1944 VPB-216, -16, and -21 were flying anti-sub and -shipping patrols out of Kossol Passage in the Palau Islands, east of the Philippines. One of 216's planes, due to some malfunctioning radar equipment, missed Kossol Passage on one of their return flights and ran out of gas.
>
> They had to ditch in open sea, and lost one pilot and several crewmen in the landing. Six remaining crew, now in the water, were kept afloat by only their life jackets in the rough water. It soon became apparent that the large fish nearby, thought at first to be porpoise, were not. They were sharks. One bit Ltjg. W. Morgan on the seat of his pants—then they knew they were in trouble.
>
> They were able to keep the sharks away for a while by splashing the water, but the animals still hung around, not far away. As the night progressed, they were bumped and bruised by sharks, and then at three A.M. one of the older sharks bit D. Chamblee, AMM [aviation machinist mate], on the left arm,

lacerating it and bringing blood. Meanwhile E. Wille, AMM, and W. Calloway, AOM [aviation ordnanceman], were clinging to a box. Calloway was butted in the rear end and he started churning backward, but recognized that discretion was the better part of valor and came back to the box and held on.

As the night ended, a rubber raft was dropped to the men. Doherty swam to get it, even though he was surrounded by sharks. Shifflet, an aviation machinist mate, helped Doherty inflate the raft. By now the sharks were getting very aggressive. One bit Shifflet on the foot. After all the men were in the raft, the sharks formed a circle around it and followed them closely until a ship arrived and picked them up. What a night! But six lucky crewmen.

## VH SQUADRONS GET THEIR MAN

It was more difficult to get information about the VH squadrons than on the VPB squadrons. Lee Roy Way, of Arlington, Texas, however, who served in VH-3 provided me with lots of good information about the history of the VH squadrons in general, and some stories about the individual squadrons.

Lee took it upon himself to write a thumbnail sketch of VH-3 operations and a brief history of all six VH units. Even though the VH squadrons got little of the notice they deserved, they had an extraordinary record in the Pacific.

*The best-looking rudder in the Navy. VPB-216 has some classy a—. (Dick Agnello photo collection)*

*VPB-216 was known for always finishing any job they started! Particularly good at metal working! (Dick Agnello photo collection)*

TOP: *VPB-216, crew 14, downed near Yap Island, awaiting rescue. They lost the plane's port float and the crew spent the night on the starboard wing to keep the plane afloat.* (Dick Agnello photo collection)

BOTTOM: *Hashmark-9 of VPB-216 at buoy and settled for the night.* (Dick Agnello photo collection)

# THE ALMOST FORGOTTEN HEROES

If the PBM was lacking in visibility in the overall campaigns of the war, the VH, or search-and-rescue, squadrons (six in total) were really low man on the totem pole. So little is known about their unique contributions that very few people have any knowledge of them. The truth is, however, they flew some of the most perilous flights of all in performing their assigned tasks.

## RESCUE SQUADRON VH-3

"Rescue Squadron VH-3 was the second of three VH units established at NAS Alameda, California, on August 1, 1944. A training syllabus program was begun using spare PBM-3Ds borrowed from FAW 8 (Fleet Air Wing 8), and in early October we were assigned six PBM-3Rs, which had been sent to England early in the war on lend-lease.

"In late October we flew the old Mariners to Kaneohe, Hawaii, to continue the training. In mid-December we left Kaneohe, flying on west to Eniwetok Atoll, and then on to Saipan, an island in the Marianas (based at Tanapag Harbor, on the northwest side of Saipan), where our rescue operations began in early January 1945.

"During flight operations from Tanapag, Saipan, we lost two Mariners on January 17 and 20 while the squadron was grounded. A review board determined the cause of the crashes.

"Six crews returned to Kaneohe, where six more PBM-3Rs were available, and flew them back to Saipan. During the time when our squadron being grounded, two of the grounded seaplanes were overhauled by CASU-48 and several missions were flown during the invasion of Iwo Jima.

"On the night of March 28, our squadron flew north from Tanapag, Saipan, arriving early on the following morning at Kerama-retto, the newly secured island ring fourteen miles off the southwestern shores of Okinawa. That same afternoon the first search-and-rescue mission was flown, which found nothing.

"From March 29, 1945, until August 13, VH-3 made 77 rescues from Kerama-retto and Buckner Bay, rescuing 175 survivors in 77 open-sea landings and 74 takeoffs. (Three times, the aircraft was damaged so extensively on landing that they had to taxi back to base on the open sea: for 145 miles, for 154 miles, and for over 200 miles.) Also, during this time, over 54 survivors were rescued by surface vessels and lifeguard submarines, when sea conditions were too heavy for our Dumbos to effect the rescue. Every time survivors were sighted by VH-3 Dumbos, the rescue

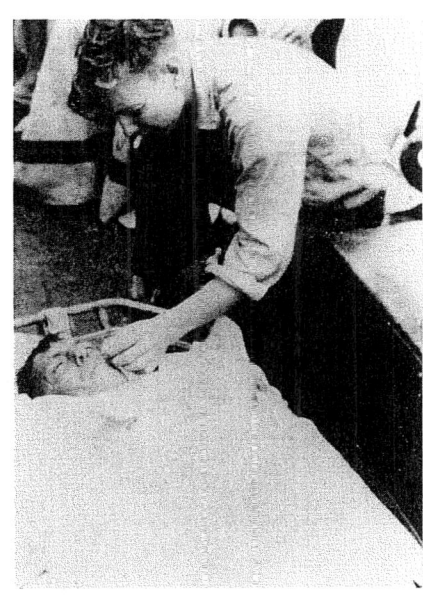

*Lee Roy Way of VH-3 lights one up for a rescued aircrew member. (VH-3 photo collection)*

or assisted rescue was made. Not one aircraft, crewman, or survivor was lost during our short history, from 1944 until 1946.

"Several of our seaplanes were removed from Navy inventory after returning to base, but the rugged Mariners always seemed to take the punishment that open-sea landings handed out. On August 13, VH-3 flew back to Tanapag, where they flew missions until returning to Kaneohe. Rescue Squadron VH-3 was disestablished on March 18, 1946. It accomplished a legacy, I feel, that is unequaled in the annals of Naval aviation history. It is very rewarding to have been a small part of the lifesaving efforts of search and rescue."

—Lee Roy Way, VH-3 combat aircrewman

## RESCUE SQUADRON VH-1

Rescue Squadron VH-1 arrived at Saipan just days after the invasion took place. PBM-5s were made available to VH squadrons in mid-April 1945. Rescue Squadron VH-2 was to be the only VH unit that could not bring their old PBM-3Rs into flying condition; they used the Catalina PB2B-2s until late in spring 1945. Rescue Squadron VH-3 was the only VH unit at Okinawa throughout the operation, with VH-1, -4, and -6, arriving in June 1945, to help in the operations at Kerama-retto and Buckner Bay. It should be noted that the USAAF emergency rescue squadrons also operated from Saipan, Iwo Jima, and Kerama-retto. Their primary role out of Saipan was responsibility for the B-29 routes to and from Japan.

## VH SQUADRONS NEVER FAIL

VH-3 was always doing the impossible. On May 12, 1944, one of their planes was making an open sea landing. This was into an eighteen-knot wind and twelve-foot waves closely grouped. The plane touched down at sixty-five knots, hitting with tremendous force. The main spars in the rear of the port and starboard engine mounts gave way, and the starboard stabilizer was damaged. In addition, the hull buckled and the port inboard flap gave way. The crew inspected the plane and they decided to taxi to the survivors and pick them up. The crew agreed and made a successful pickup. Then they decided to try a JATO takeoff—firing all four rockets at once. The plane was airborne in nine seconds, but hung in a stalled position until the pilot rolled the forward tab, praying. The plane nosed over and picked up speed, and they flew back to base.

# VH SQUADRON HISTORY

The history of VH squadrons and the Martin Mariners they used began in the Atlantic operations during convoy duties performed by PBY Catalinas and Mariners. Several times the Mariners, when seeing survivors in lifeboats or rafts after their ships had been torpedoed, successfully landed in heavy seas to effect the rescue, then took off without JATO and flew the survivors back to base.

The Navy's brain trust realized the advantage these high gull-winged Mariners had over the low-slung Catalinas in heavy sea conditions. Also, the vast expanses of the Pacific seas were beginning to be controlled by our forces, which meant a greater need of search-and-rescue. For up until early 1944, the only sea-air rescue operations in the Pacific theater were done by Catalinas, float planes, surface vessels, or lifeguard submarines.

Thus the Navy formed six squadrons whose sole purpose was search-and-rescue. Rescue squadrons 1, 3, and 5 were formed at NAS Alameda, California: Squadron VH-1 was formed in February 1944, VH-3 on August 1, and VH-5 in late September. At NAS San Diego, squadrons 2, 4 and 6 were formed. VH-2 and VH-4 began sometime between mid-August and mid September 1944; VH-6 in January 1945.

Each VH unit had a twofold mission. The PBMs would carry out the search-and-rescue mission, and each squadron would also have six R4D-5s, for patient evacuation.

The Navy, realizing the management and displacement problem of two totally different functions, equipped evacuation

*A B-25 bomber crew picked up by one of VH-3's planes. (Lee Roy Way photo collection)*

squadrons VH-1, VH-2, and VH-3 with land planes in addition to their PBMs. VH-2 and VH-3 used the R4D-5s as planned for land maneuvers; but VH-1 used PB2Ys instead. These three evacuation squadrons amassed a tremendous record in flying the wounded from battlefields to rear-area hospitals, saving many lives.

*This Quonset hut was office, meeting room, and duty station while VPB-28 was operating from Jinamoc in 1945. (VPB-28 photo collection)*

TOP: *Norm Lorentzsen, VPB-21, crew 1, lectures on moderation in all things in this life. (Source unknown)*

BOTTOM: *VPB-25 personnel off to morning chow at the local tropical eatery run by the U.S Navy. (Source unknown)*

TOP: *Norm Lorentzsen, PPC, crew 1, VPB-21, on the radar dome of V-1. (Don Kramer photo collection)*

BOTTOM: *Scotch was a little hard to find at Palau, so cocktail hour's theme was "Coca-Cola is the one for you." (Art Kennedy photo collection)*

TOP: *Loading bombs onto a repaired PBM. (Source unknown)*

BOTTOM: *VPB-27's E-11 gassing up from an AVP. (Dick Gingrich photo collection)*

*Two guys ready to go backward into battle: tail gunners from (top) VPB-16 and (bottom) VPB-216. (Dick Agnello photo collection)*

TOP: *Crew 14, VPB-21, drops a bomb that hits directly on a pier and four barges. (VPB-21 Crew 14 photo collection)*

BOTTOM: *Cleaning a waist gun at Kerama-retto—a buoy-watch task. (Source unknown)*

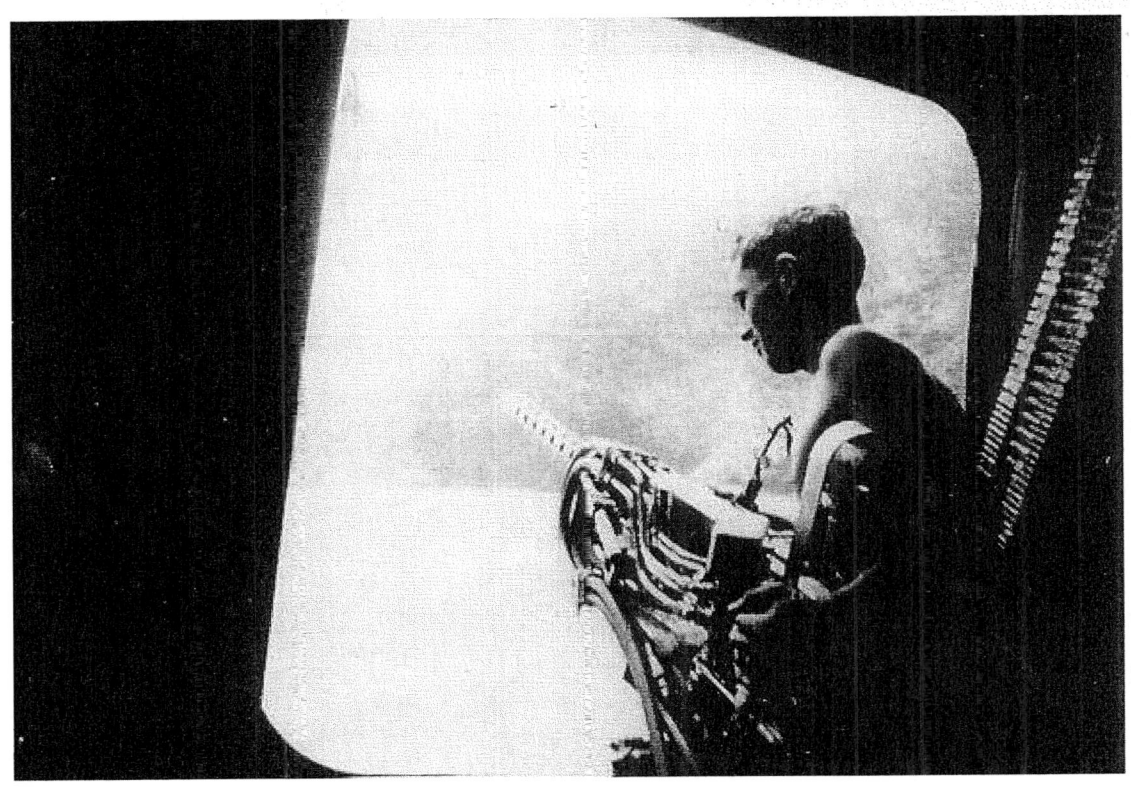

TOP: *Crew 14 VPB-21 attacks and sinks a Japanese lugger off the coast of Korea.* (USS Chandeleur *photo collection*)

BOTTOM: *A Sugar Dog about to be attacked by a VPB-21 Mariner.* (*VPB-21 Crew 14 photo collection*)

TOP: *"Bombs away!" V-14 of VPB-21 attacks a pier, a Sugar Dog, and several luggers. (USS* Chandeleur *photo collection)*

BOTTOM: *Following up VPB-21 V-14's bombing of a pier... a strafing run on the same targets. (USS* Chandeleur *photo collection)*

The Men and Their Squadrons   111

*A Japanese freighter, under attack off the coast of Korea, desperately tries to hide in one of the innumerable small bays or coves. See also, next photo. (Source unknown)*

*The Japanese freighter attacked in the previous photo is left heavily damaged and smoking. (Source unknown)*

*A Japanese gunboat under way and under attack from a VPB-208 plane. (Harvey Herzog photo collection)*

TOP: *Crews 14 and 16, VPB-21, attack a small Japanese bulk carrier. Both planes were hit by small-caliber antiaircraft fire. A couple of gutsy Japanese guys, one back by the bridge and one forward by the hatch covers, are trying to avoid the strafing of the Mariners. (VPB-21 Crews 14 and 16 photo collections.)*

BOTTOM: *The ship eventually sank. With wounded crewmen aboard V-16 and damaged controls on V-14, both planes made it back to base. The wounds were not life threatening, so all in all it was a favorable day for VPB-21. (VPB-21 Crews 14 and 16 photo collections.)*

BELOW: *Japanese mine layer about forty miles out of Shanghai and about to be attacked by V-14 and V-18 of VPB-21. (USS* Chandeleur *photo collection)*

FACING PAGE, TOP: *A Sugar Dog about to get a barrage from one VPB-21's Mariners just off the coast of Korea. (USS* Chandeleur *photo collection)*

FACING PAGE, BOTTOM: *VPB-21's crew 16 sinks a Sugar Dog, May 1945 in the China Sea. (VPB-21 Crew 16 photo collection)*

TOP: *A Japanese Jill fighter downed near Aguni-shima. (VPB-21 Crew 14 photo collection).*

BOTTOM: *Kusakaki-shima's radio-radar installation is bombed. (USS* Chandeleur *photo collection)*

TOP: *Attack on a lighthouse and radar station in southern Japan, April 27, 1945. (Source unknown)*

BOTTOM: *A Sugar Dog going under in the China Sea, courtesy of the crew of V-4 from VPB-21, August 4, 1945. And it's almost over!* (USS Chandeleur *photo collection*)

BELOW (2 PHOTOS): *Sugar Dog under way. "Now you see it, now you don't." Crew 7, VPB-21, is at it again. June 1945. (VPB-21 Crew 7 photo collection)*

*Two Sugar Dogs being attacked by a VPB-21 Mariner in the South China Sea. (USS* Chandeleur *photo collection)*

BELOW AND FACING PAGE, TOP (3 PHOTOS): *Three views of a Sugar Dog under fire by a Mariner from VPB-21, crew 14. May 1945. (Source unknown)*

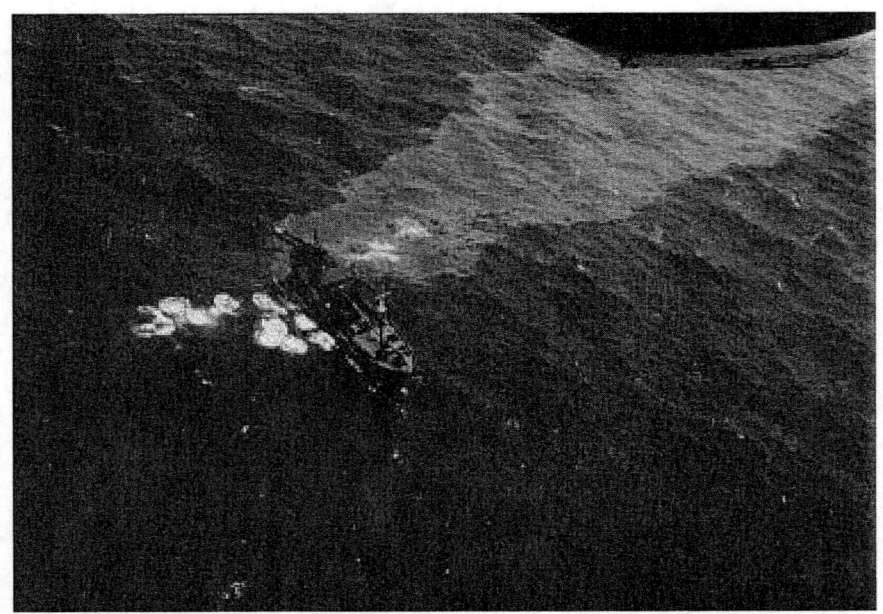

BELOW: *Another Sugar Dog goes under. VPB-21, crew 7. June 10, 1945.*

TOP: *A VPB-27 Mariner hit by a 40mm shell on the starboard side. This photo shows where the shell entered. See also the next photo. (Bill Ferrall photo collection)*

BOTTOM: *The shell went through the Mariner and out the port side without exploding. Lucky day! See also the previous photo. (Bill Ferrall photo collection)*

TOP: *A. D. Brown, of VPB-21's crew 6, checking 20mm holes in the rudder of V-6 after running battle with George fighters. (USS* Chandeleur *photo collection)*

BOTTOM: *A VPB-27 E-2 being hurried aboard its tender after battle with a Japanese convoy. (Bill Ferrall photo collection)*

*Crew 12, VPB-21, downed between Eniwetok and Wake. All were rescued; two were injured—one pilot and one aviation machinist spent a day and night with sharks until picked up by a destroyer escort. (VPB-21 Crew 6 photo collection)*

# THE SHIPS

*The USS* Hamlin. *(Jay Broze photo collection)*

# CHANGING ROLES

World War II changed forever the concept of how to utilize certain types of ships, both old and new. Actually, I believe that it was the aircraft carrier that was affected the most, by allowing the airplane to reach an enemy's ships or shore installations with less risk to other ships.

Seaplane tenders played a nvery significant role in the new concept of amphibious warfare in the Pacific. As discussed earlier, the tenders were often in the vanguard of the invasion fleet. The seaplanes became important as the eyes of the fleet and performed flying feats never expected from a big, slow, gull-winged airplane. It even amazed those of us who flew them and in them how the PBMs could handle torpedo attacks, bombing raids, Black Catting, and more.

The tenders were not officially listed as combat ships. But they in some instances arrived at an invasion site three to four days before D-day landings. Tenders provided all the essentials to accommodate the aircrews—meals, sleeping quarters (as such), and other necessities. Their primary mission, however, was to provide major repairs, as routine maintenance was usually accomplished on the water, working on aluminum work platforms hooked to the plane's leading edge of the wings.

*The USS* Curtiss. *(Bill Ferrall photo collection)*

## CLASSES OF TENDERS

There were basically two classes of tenders: AV and AVP. The AVs ranged from the Currituck class, at 15,092 tons, to the Curtiss class, at 13,777 tons, that had a crane on the aft deck (the seaplane deck), which allowed a plane to be brought on board for maintenance and repair. The Curtiss and Currituck classes could handle two planes at once. The AVPs, Barnegat class at 2800 tons, could not service planes on board.

The greatest congregation of seaplane tenders and seaplane squadrons ever assembled was at Kerama-retto during the battle of Okinawa. The tenders arrived three days before actual D-day. There were twelve—five AVs (with an average crew of 1,010) and seven AVPs (with an average crew of 294)—tending 111 seaplanes. The AVs were: USS *St. George,* USS *Chandeleur,* USS *Hamlin,* USS *Yakutat,* and USS *Norton Sound.* The AVPs were USS *Onslow,* USS *Shelikof,* USS *Mackinac,* USS *Suisun,* USS *Kenneth Whiting,* USS *Casco,* USS *Bering Strait.*

The tenders operating in the other areas of the southwest Pacific were the AVs USS *Currituck,* USS *Pocomoke,* and USS

*The USS* Hamlin *under way. (Jay Broze photo collection)*

TOP: *An AVP fueling two Mariners at Leyte Bay, Philippines. (Bill Ferrall photo collection)*

BOTTOM: *The USS* Mackinac *at anchor in Kerama-retto, July 1945. (Lee Roy Way photo collection)*

TOP: *Dog Victor 4 of VPB-21 ready to get under way at Kerama-retto. Fred Dickey, copilot, looks out the window. (Lee Orsak photo collection)*

BOTTOM: *The USS* Chandeleur, *AV-10, tied up at Saipan, August 1944. (Don Sweet photo collection)*

TOP: *The USS* Shelikof. *(Bill Ferrall photo collection)*

BOTTOM: *The USS* Shelikof *(AVP) at anchor in Kerama-retto. (Source unknown)*

*Tangier*; and the AVPs USS *Half Moon*, USS *Barataria*, USS *San Pablo*, and USS *Duxbury Bay*.

## JONAH IN THE WHALE

Father Early, a former combat aircrewman who is with a monastery in western Connecticut and was in VPB-20, wrote me and put another spin on tender life.

> While reading your book, The Sailor Aviators, *many past images began to arise in my head, especially those of being aboard the seaplane tenders. I often had to hunt around on the small destroyerlike tenders for a bunk to sleep in. The "hot bunk" system existed on four of the five tenders we were living on, and oftentimes we had to sleep out on deck because of the overcrowded conditions.*
>
> *In relation to the typhoons, I give a talk, which is entitled "In the Belly of the Whale." I refer to the Old Testament of Jonah, being in the belly of the whale and how it had great effect on him. Then I proceed to describe our two-day typhoon ordeal that one fine day affected the entire ship.*

## THE PATSUs

The key to the tenders' existence was really the PATSU (patrol aircraft service unit). This was in simple terms the maintenance group, and they did a magnificent job. The ship I was on, the *Chandeleur*, in their first eighteen months of operations in the Pacific sent out 2,075 flights for missions and missed but one due to maintenance difficulties. That does not mean they did not work around the clock at times! A lot of their work was on a plane's portable maintenance platform, so mechanics had to hold on with one hand and work with the other.

The problem of maintenance was compounded by the environment—the salt water. Theoretically, a seaplane needs about three hours of maintenance for every hour flown. Engines needed complete overhaul or replacement every hundred to one hundred fifty hours of flying time.

The tender maintenance record has to be second to none—incredible, in light of the obstacles. We often joked that they were too good. In bad flying weather, we'd hope they couldn't fix some problem, but off we'd go because they never let us miss a flight, weather or no weather!

*A U.S. destroyer backs away from the USS* Chandeleur *after delivering the mail. (Jim Guay photo collection)*

## THE AVPs

Throughout the Okinawa campaign VPB-27 was based on two AVPs. Many problems arose from this distribution of personnel, since six crews were aboard each ship. The job of coordinating flight schedules and maintenance work, at times, seemed insurmountable. But the willing cooperation of all hands, and extra effort on the part of the tenders, resulted in a workable solution to all problems. All routine maintenance was performed by maintenance crews on the water, and the only time planes were hoisted onto an AV was for major repairs.

The flight schedule was so heavy that it was necessary for the AVP's PATSU to do major maintenance, for example, to make the hundred-twenty-hour checks on water. Somehow it always got done and usually on time!

TOP: *A U.S. submarine off the coast of Formosa, May 1945. Subs would be in the areas for which bombers would head when hit by antiaircraft fire. The PBMs would then direct the sub to where parachuting survivors were landing. (Frank L. Hannig photo collection)*

BOTTOM: *A whaleboat heads for its AVP with buoy-watch change. (Bill Ferrall photo collection)*

134   Seaplanes at War

TOP: *A disabled Japanese freighter in Tanapag Harbor, Saipan. It was a good landmark in inclement weather. (George Lindberg photo collection)*

BOTTOM: *A U.S. destroyer picks up crew 14 of VPB-216 near Yap Island, July 1944. (Dick Agnello photo collection)*

TOP: *Mail call soon. . . . Mail arrives aboard the USS Chandeleur. (S. E. Karp photo collection)*

BOTTOM: *Working off all that "good chow" with a hot game of volleyball on the USS Tangier. (Jim Guay photo collection)*

TOP: *Looks like a girl, smells like a girl, feels like a girl . . . it is a girl!!! Frances Langford, movie actress on a USO tour to the Far East. (Don Kramer photo collection)*

BOTTOM: *The* Chandeleur's *air force on the seaplane deck— "Grumman Duck." (Fred Dickey photo collection)*

*Broadway comes to the USS Hamlin—all hands on deck! Christmas 1945. (USS* Hamlin *photo collection)*

# THE WAR ENDS

*A section of Nagasaki after the bomb. As you can see, only a few buildings were left standing. (Doc Doherty photo collection)*

*This photo of the imperial palace, in Tokyo, shows no damage from the U.S. bombs that destroyed the rest of city (the palace was off limits). (Doc Doherty photo collection)*

## OVERVIEW

At last it was over, and the timing was great for me, as I was just about ready to head back for the planned invasion of the Japanese mainland. The two atomic bombs, however, finally made the point to the governing Japanese that they could not win this war.

It was interesting to me that we had destroyed so many of their cities with conventional bombing, but it took the A-bombs to push them over the edge. It has to have been the fact that this bomb killed eighty thousand people at one crack, as opposed to the huge number of regular raids it would have taken to accomplish the same level of destruction.

## SURPRISE, SURPRISE

War is full of surprises, and our adversaries, the Japanese, were masters of surprise. Generally, these are things that provide a more efficient way to kill. There are occasions, however, when it is something that is so bizarre it's hard to believe.

That's what the kamikaze concept did to the American psyche. Even after some fifty-seven years, I find it hard to comprehend a loyalty that would cause me to voluntarily kill myself in deference to my leader. The concept of the word *surrender* was not even allowed to be considered. The belief being, that honorable suicide is better than defeat. That makes for a difficult opponent!

*A view of Nagasaki, showing debris and emptiness after the U.S. atomic bomb was dropped here. (Source unknown)*

## SUICIDE AS A WEAPON

I view this use of suicide as a weapon as a concept that evolved out of the Bushido military tradition of self-sacrifice. I saw it spelled out years ago in Richard O'Neill's book, *Suicide Squads*:

> *The tradition of self-sacrifice was loyalty to the Emperor (believed to be a god), then loyalty to feudal lords, then to the nation, and then the individual. What was so scary about this idea was that the individual knew it was his duty to die. As the war went on, it was obvious that the pool of well-trained aviators was minimal, so it was a perfect situation for the Japanese, as the training of a kamikaze pilot was only a week long.*

Basically, they were taught how to aim their plane at a target and hope that the collision between the two would explode the gasoline and any ordnance carried. This was acceptable as honorable, although it was not the traditional method of Bushido suicide (disembowelment was the traditional way). It is bizarre to me, as I said, that a week of concentrated training on getting the plane to a target to inflict the maximum damage and kill oneself was acceptable to anyone—pilot or emperor.

Interestingly, I really don't believe that we initially thought the Japanese were anything more than a barbaric, backward,

*George fighter planes during a kamikaze attack on the stern of the USS* Hamlin, *which is the ship in the center of the photo. This photo has ben enhanced slightly. (Jay Broze photo collection)*

idol-worshiping country. Lots of people felt at the time that if they started a war, it would be over in three or four weeks. But when the war finally started, most of my peers and their families believed that the Japanese were invincible: the Japanese fighter plane, the Zero, was unbeatable, and the Japanese soldier was the best jungle fighter in the world. Those beliefs seemed to be justified, at first, on the basis of enemy conquests—the list of which grew each day.

The horror of the kamikaze is personified by this story. On May 6, 1945, an enemy Tony fighter plane dove into the seaplane

*The first kamikaze hit the* Hamlin *(in center of photo) on its seaplane deck. Several other kamikazes took antiaircraft hits. That is why many of the planes in this photo appear blurred. This photo has ben enhanced slightly. (Jay Broze photo collection)*

TOP: *A photo of contrasts in Nagasaki: on the near side of the river things look fairly normal; on the far side, complete devastation reigns. (Source unknown)*

BOTTOM: *Japanese soldiers captured in Kerama-retto by a crew from the USS* Chandeleur *and VPB-21. (USS* Chandeleur *photo collection)*

deck of the USS *St. George*, hitting at the base of the crane. The engine of the plane carried through three decks of heavy steel, crashing into the stateroom of two VPB-18 PPCs: Lt. Jordan Collins and Lt. Peter Prudden. Collins was killed instantly and Prudden was seriously burned by the fire that ensued. One of the squadron's enlisted personnel suffered some minor injuries. It amazed me that it went through three steel decks. . . . Nothing was a safe haven!

*The next six pages show Japanese envoys arriving at Ieshima in white Betty bombers, then boarding a U.S. plane to continue on to Philippines, where they will arrange for the Japanese surrender. (Bill Ferrall photo collection)*

TOP: *The first Betty (medium bomber) to land on Allied soil without receiving an antiaircraft barrage . . . (Bill Ferrall photo collection)*

BOTTOM: *Taxiiing past an armed guard . . . one of whom probably would like to practice his sharpshooting. (Bill Ferrall photo collection)*

TOP: *No formal reception here . . . it was wise of the Japanese to quickly reboard and leave the area.* (Bill Ferrall photo collection)

BOTTOM: *A Betty parked in a secure area of the field, with armed guards.* (Bill Ferrall photo collection)

TOP: *Doesn't look like too happy a group.... Some guys felt it would be nice if they all went to jail. (Bill Ferrall photo collection)*

BOTTOM: *At least they aren't flying first class! Some Americans might have advised them to check their luggage for bombs—but then, it would have been a shame to lose a perfectly good C-54! (Bill Ferrall photo collection)*

# THE BOMB

The atomic bomb was a device that up to that time existed only in the minds of the funny-looking "doctors" in comic strips such as Flash Gordon (Dr. Zarkhov) or Buck Rogers. Now it was real, and the destructive power was beyond our imaginations. In a flash it destroyed a large city, and the aftereffects lingered long after the actual attack was over.

But after they were dropped, we could go home if we were lucky. I, like a lot of other people, was lucky. Unfortunately, too many of my generation died, and I just hope that the future tells us it was all worth it.

*A section of Nagasaki that, after the bomb, had next to nothing left standing. (Source unknown)*

# DEMOCRACY AWAKES

But back to the fighting: everything began to change in our favor once industry got cranked up. Then the horrendous battle of Midway was the icing on the cake, as was the beginning of the demise of Japanese air power as a result of the "Marianas turkey shoot." Overall, the tremendous losses of planes and pilots began to convince even the hardest hardliners that all was not going well. It may also have been the impetus for Japan's building up its suicide squads for kamikaze flights and *kikusui* attacks.

As noted in my book, *The Sailor Aviators,* an unprecedented order of magnitude of a kamikaze's success would be reflected in the period April 6 to June 22, 1945, when kamikazes sank 11 ships and damaged 102. On the seventh of April alone, about 350 kamikazes, with another 350 planes, attacked in the Okinawa area. They sank three destroyers, a landing-ship tank, and two ammunition ships while damaging twenty-four other ships. Not too bad a day.

## APOLOGY?

I feel personally compelled to insert some editorial comments here to counter some of the so-called revisionists who are second-guessing so many of the decisions of World War II. There are always any number of "experts" who usually have no personal knowledge but are full of their own expertise. I am still disgusted after all these years when I recall the beheading of our captured fliers by the Japanese or the incineration of our POWs in gasoline-filled trenches. Why this constant harping about the use of the atomic bomb?

I suggest that people read *The Rape of Nanking* by Iris Chang, in which is recounted how the Japanese raped, tortured, and murdered over three hundred thousand Chinese in Nanking alone. Through all of this, there has never been a hint of an apology from Japan.

I personally am offended at the brazen forgetfulness of a nation that prides itself on its philosophies of democracy and justice for all.

War and the heat of battle do indeed bring out the worst in man, and we are not lily-white in light of some of the activities that we perpetuated during those years. But we did nothing on the scale of the above.

## THE LAST WORD

There were many individual surrender ceremonies; various squadrons played a role in them. For example, VPB-21 dropped the surrender or armistice papers on Wake Island and Ponape as part of the overall armistice signed aboard the USS *Missouri* in Tokyo Bay.

# A TOUGH AND HOMELY OLD BIRD

I have long been a noisy ex–sailor aviator about PBMs. I have always felt that the PBM was tough, homely, and relatively unknown among the "more glamorous" planes of World War II. I personally do not know of a more versatile plane in terms of absorbing punishment, or one that was as flexible vis-à-vis the missions undertaken.

Five examples of combat success are spelled out below. They are good examples of the value of the PBM in the Pacific war. I have not intended to slight any of the sailor aviators of the fifteen other squadrons that flew during this period of time in the Pacific battleground, but rather I have used representative information that was both available and most probably accurate.

VPB-18, flying in the central Pacific, racked up a fine record of 34 ships sunk, 12 planes shot down, and many aggressive attacks on ground installations.

VPB-20, flying the in the southwest Pacific, had an unbelievable 44 ships sunk and 32 damaged (128,000 tons), as well as 2 planes shot down and 24 air-sea rescues.

VPB-21, flying in the central Pacific, logged 14,000 flight hours of combat missions. It sank 12 ships and damaged 32; had 1 confirmed submarine sinking, 1 submarine heavily damaged, and 3 submarine kill assists; 3 planes "confirmed"; numerous bombings of ground targets.

VPB-27 sank 21 ships and damaged 11 while flying ASW patrols and antishipping missions at Okinawa that totaled 10,245.7 hours.

VPB-28 sank or damaged some 42 ships (76,950 tons were sunk; 43,910 tons damaged). Its average mission time was 12.7 hours.

The above are records hard to ignore: for just five of the twenty-one PBM squadrons there were 138 ships sunk! A record that all PBM sailor aviators can always be proud of.

*VPB-21 Mariner at buoy off Parry Island, Eniwetok, August 1944. (Norm Lorentzsen photo collection)*

*A PBM-5 "on the step" during a takeoff run on Middle River at the Glenn L. Martin manufacturing plant, Baltimore, Maryland. (courtesy of the Glenn L. Martin Company)*

*A good perspective on flying a mission in a PBM was put into verse by John Sugrue in VPB-26 and reprinted here from a Mariner/Marlin newsletter.*

# Come Fly With Me

The hour is early; sun's over the horizon the day almost whole.
The crew assembles with gear and ration
To begin once more a combat patrol.
Now it's into the boat with a well-timed leap;
Carelessness here means physical pain.
Out to the plane, which looks awkward and weak
While still imprisoned by its briny chains.
Slowly it plows through the adhering water
Till permission is given, and it's ready to fly.
Then full power on, throwing spray to each quarter,
It lumbers and shudders as if to die.
Bouncing and jouncing from one wave to the next
Straining metal and man almost to the limit,
She tears through the water at a speed breakneck
Trying to break the attraction of it.
The ride finally smooths as she rides up on the step,
Clipping each wave right at the top.
Then one final bounce gives her extra pep
And it's into the air, shedding many a drop.
She looks ungainly as she struggles for height
That changes slowly as picks up speed.
Soaring gracefully she is quite a sight,
True and dependable as a bold knight's steed.
The flight is long—twelve hours or more
Looking over a sea of innumerable waves
Or carefully following some foreign shore
Or watching the clouds from lofty caves.
Boredom, an enemy, is always present.
Ruthless and strong, it will test our mettle.
But we fly on to fill our intent,
To find the enemy and press the battle.
The hours pass and we start our descent
To the friendly waters of our home base,
Happy to see it's till extant.
It isn't much, but it is our place.
Now back to the ship for food and rest,
A nice clean bunk, and a hot shower.
We've given our all and done our best.
This combat patrol is finally over.

*The usual "smooth water" at Kossol Passage. (George Lindberg photo collection)*

*"There are no flowers on a sailor's grave"—from an old German sailor song. (Jay Broze photo collection)*

# EPILOGUE

I have always looked for the perfect words to say about PBM squadrons of the Pacific war, and borrowing from some of the accolades of varied squadrons, I wrote the following to all of our shipmates of the Patrol Bombing Squadrons flying the venerable Martin Mariner, the PBM.

> For outstanding heroism in action against enemy Japanese forces from January 1944 to August 1945. Patrol Bombing Squadrons flying the Martin Mariner PBM seaplane maintained flights with persistent determination despite the hazards of heavy enemy antiaircraft fire and hostile fighter opposition to destroy hundreds of thousands of tons of vital Japanese shipping and to inflict severe damage on more hundreds of thousands of tons more. They sank or damaged a score of submarines and destroyed or damaged enemy aircraft. Individually heroic and aggressive, the pilots and aircrewmen flew in support of all major offensive activities during this eighteen-month period.
>
> This valiant record of combat in missions excellently planned and executed was made possible only by the courage, skill, and superb teamwork of the pilots, the flight crews, and the men who serviced and maintained the planes. Their perseverance, high standards of achievement, and unwavering devotion to duty reflected the highest credit upon the PBM patrol bombing squadrons of the United States naval service.

*Crew 2 of VPB-27 came across this B-29 bomber north of Saipan. It was intact, and the crew was rescued from their life rafts. The plane broke in half after the rescue. One last crewman was found there just hanging on to the outboard port engine! (Bill Ferrall photo collection)*

*Vance Kyle, crew 10, VPB-17, receives his air medal. Admiral to Lance, "Son I assume you are a tail gunner." (Vance Kyle photo collection)*

# Key Contributors
## To This Story Are:

The Turner Publishing Company and their book, *Mariner/Marlin Anywhere, Anytime,* and the generosity of Dave Turner, president. This book is a compilation of many, many former PBM crewmen remembrances, squadron histories from Naval archives and individual squadrons, and many of my own experiences.

The fine personal support and assistance provided by the Mariner/Marlin Association— and their chairman, Richard Gingrich, their newsletter editor, Dave Rinehart, and their historian, Bruce Barth.

Invaluable assistance came from Lee Roy Way of VH-3 about the Dumbo squadrons.

Then Bill Ferrall of VPB-27 and Jay Broze VPB-208, without whom this book would not exist.

I would be very remiss if I did not recognize Diana Donovan, publisher, Celo Valley Books, who was absolutely invaluable for as poor a grammarian/writer as I.

Two people who supported me with encouragement and interest ... George and Alex Kalivas, owners of Il Vilino. This Italian restaurant is the best.

Individual contributors were many, and I am sure I missed some of them as I built the following list. I can only apologize if I overlooked you and I am sorry; but a book is never compiled by one person, but by many people. I am very aware that I could not ever have done any of my books by myself.

Bill Silver, historian

James Sawruk, Naval historian

*Spud Pinkney (VPB-205) exhibiting his many artistic abilities (?) on the side of his plane. (Spud Pinkney photo collection)*

VPB-17
  Tom Russell
  Frank Dunigan
  Vance Kyle
  Leon Roberts

VPB-18
  Don Graham
  Harvey Herzog
  Jim Lodge

TOP: *Left: F. Dickey, VPB-21, crew 4 pilot; Right: Lee Orsak, VPB-21, crew 14 pilot. (Source unknown)*

BOTTOM: *Bob Shaw, VPB-21, crew 9, plane captain. (Robert F. Shaw photo collection)*

VPB-19
 George Lindberg
 Dick Agnello

VP-20
 Carl Horton
 Bernard Leonard
 Wayne Byerly
 Mike Cox

VPB-21
 Don Kramer
 John Hook
 B. J. Mountain
 James Guay
 Fred Dickey
 Jack Darbyshire
 Dan Durda
  (son of Joe Durda,
  PPC Crew 14)
 Jeanne Powers
  (widow of R. B. Powers)
 Dick Simms
 Chad Alger
 Ellie Alger
  (wife of Chad Alger)
 Art Kennedy
 Bob Peyton
 Lee Orsak

VPB-22
 Bob Willig

VPB-26
 Russ Mattes
 Dick Brodeur

VPB-27
 Bill Ferrall
 Dick Gingrich

VPB-28
 Bob Van Trieste
 Frank Hannig

VPB-45
 Charles Caldwell

VPB-202
 William Kreitzer

VPB-205
 "Spud" Pinkney
VPB-208
 Jay Broze
 Walter Schurman

VPB-216
 Dick Agnello
 "Doc" Doherty
 Dick Gingrich

VH-3
 Lee Roy Way

TOP: *What well-dressed airman are wearing this year (1944)! Left: B. J. Mountain, VPB-21, crew 7 pilot; right: P. E. Casey, VPB-21, crew 14 pilot. (Don Sweet photo collection)*

BOTTOM: *Burke, Kyle, and (?) of VPB-17 on Luzon June 1945. Kyle tipped the scales at a hefty 103 pounds! (Vance Kyle photo collection)*

TOP: *Lt. Joe Durda, VPB-21, PPC of crew 14. A great guy, "one of the men of war." (Dan Durda photo collection)*

BOTTOM: *Bill Ferrall and a couple of his buddies from VPB-208 passing a quiet afternoon. (Bill Ferrall photo collection)*

*ARM2c Harvey Herzog, VPB-18, gets his air medal. "Another one of the men of war." (Source unknown)*

*VPB-216's Bob Smith's plane headed home, November 1944, with the usual graffiti and the only shark mouth in fleet! (Bob Smith photo collection)*

# GLOSSARY

| | |
|---|---|
| AA | Antiaircraft fire; also called flak. |
| aircrewmen | Enlisted personnel who constitute a PBM crew, along with three or four pilots. They are aviation machinist mates, ordnancemen, and radiomen. |
| airedales | Nickname given aviators/aircrews by shipboard sailors. |

airplanes—
  American, Navy:

| | |
|---|---|
| F4U | Corsair, Navy and Marine fighter |
| F6F | Hellcat, Navy carrier fighter |
| OS2U | Kingfisher, Navy scout observation plane |
| PB2Y | Coronado, Navy patrol bomber |
| PB4Y | Navy version of the Liberator bomber |
| PBM | Mariner, Navy patrol bomber |
| PBY | Catalina, Navy patrol bomber |
| SB2C | Helldiver, Navy dive bomber |
| TBF | Avenger torpedo bomber |

  American, Army:

| | |
|---|---|
| B-24 | Liberator, Army Air Force heavy bomber |
| B-25 | Mitchell, Army Air Force medium bomber |
| B-29 | Superfortress, Army Air Force heavy bomber |
| P-51 | Mustang, Army Air Force fighter |

  Japanese:

| | |
|---|---|
| Betty | Mitsubishi medium bomber |
| Emily | Patrol seaplane |
| Francis | Fighter bomber |
| George | Fighter |
| Tojo | Fighter |
| Val | Aichi 99, dive bomber |
| Aldis lamp | Signal light for visual communication |
| AMM | Aviation machinist mate. |
| AOM | Aviation ordnanceman. |

| | |
|---|---|
| ARM | Aviation radioman. |
| ASP | Anti-submarine patrol. |
| ASW | Anti-submarine warfare. |
| Bendix transmitter | Radio |
| Black Cat | PBY painted black for night attacks. See also: Nightmare. |
| black shoes | Nickname for shipboard sailors. |
| boot camp | Basic training for servicemen. |
| BOQ | Bachelor officer quarters. |
| brown shoes | Nickname for naval aviators. |
| buoy | A circular float with metal rings used to tie planes to on the water when no ramp facilities were available. |
| CAP | Combat Air Patrol. (Fighter planes that flew air cover over ships at sea and over island bases.) |
| chief | Senior grade of petty officer; e.g., chief aviation machinist mate, chief aviation radioman, etc. |
| Cincpac | Commander in Chief Pacific Fleet |
| classified submarine patrol zone | Safe area for U.S. submarines |
| CO | Commanding Officer. |
| ComNorPac | Commander North Pacific fleet. |
| ComSubPac | Commander Submarines Pacific |
| chow | Food. |
| crash crew | A crew available to go to crash scenes to do whatever needed doing. |
| cumshaw | A nice word for stolen goods. See also: midnight small stores. |
| D-day | The day, usually unspecified, set for the beginning of a planned attack. |
| D-Day | The day the Allies began the invasion of western Europe, by invading at Normandy Beach: June 6, 1944. |
| deck | Floor. |
| dive bomber | An airplane of the fighter-bomber type that drops its bombs while diving at the enemy. |
| Dumbo | Air-sea rescue plane. |
| fantail | Rearmost deck of ship. |
| FAW | Fleet Air Wing. |
| flak | *See:* AA. |

gedunk . . . . . . . Ice cream.
Geographical terms:
  English words:
    atoll . . . . . . . A coral island consisting of a reef surrounding a lagoon
    archipelago . . . A group of islands, often in a chain formation.
    reef . . . . . . A chain of rocks or coral, or a ridge of sand at or near the surface of the water. In this text it is often used in reference to the coral makeup of an island (as opposed to sand), that is not, however, shaped to surround a lagoon, like an atoll.
  Foreign words:
    gunto (Japanese) archipelago
    jima (Japanese) island
    kai (Japanese) sea
    retto (Japanese) island chain
    shima (Japanese) island
    shoto (Japanese) archipelago
    tao (Chinese) island
    to (Japanese) island
    wan (Chinese, Japanese) bay, gulf

GO-9 transmitter . . . Powerful radio transmitter on PBM-3D.
GQ . . . . . . . . General Quarters. An alert sounded when action was pending. A warning to man battle stations.
Gibson girl . . . . . Emergency radio set carried on life rafts.
head . . . . . . . . Bathroom facilities.
Hedron . . . . . . Headquarters organization for a number of squadrons; e.g., Hedron 5-1 is Headquarters Squadron 5-1.
IFF . . . . . . . . Identification Friend or Foe—an electronic signal device to identify friendly planes. The specific signal was changed daily.
intercom . . . . . . Internal radio communication system on plane.
intervolameter . . . . A device used to set the distance between bombs to be dropped.

| | |
|---|---|
| JATO | Jet-assisted takeoff. |
| *kaiten* | Japanese suicide torpedo boat. The *kaiten* was shaped like a mini-sub, with the torpedo taking up most of the "ship," and a small control room in the front for the captain. The captain would steer the torpedo toward the target. The whole thing would explode on impact. |
| kamikaze | Japanese suicide bomber. Also used to refer to the pilot of such a plane. |
| *kikusui* | A massed kamikaze attack, used to maximize effectiveness. There were 10 *kikusui* (literally, "floating chrysanthemum") attacks, dating from April 6, 1945–June 22, 1945. |
| knot | Measurement of ship or air speed; one knot is equal to one nautical mile per hour. |
| ladder | Stairs. |
| LST | Landing ship tank: an amphibious ship. |
| Mae West | Inflatable life jacket worn by all plane crew. |
| mark | An ordnance designator, e.g., Mark 47 depth charge, Mark 18 torpedo, Mark VIII gun sight. |
| mess hall | Military eating facility. |
| mess tent | Same as a mess hall, only in a tent instead of in a building. |
| mission | A patrol seeking: location of the enemy, weather information, etc. |
| NAAS | Naval Auxiliary Air Station. |
| napalm | A highly incendiary jellylike substance used in fire bombs, flamethrowers, etc. |
| NAS | Naval Air Station. |
| NATS | Naval Air Transport Service. A service provided by naval planes assigned to carry cargo, mail, passengers, and the like. |
| Nightmare | PBM painted black for night attacks. See also: Black Cat. |

Officers
- American Navy:
  - Adm. . . . . . . Admiral
  - Capt. . . . . . . Captain
  - Cdr. . . . . . . Commander
  - Ens. . . . . . . Ensign
  - Lcdr. . . . . . . Lieutenant Commander
  - Lt. . . . . . . . Lieutenant
  - Ltjg. . . . . . . Lieutenant, Junior Grade
  - Radm. . . . . . Rear Admiral

OOD . . . . . . . . Officer of the day.

PA . . . . . . . . . Public address system.
passageway . . . . . Hall or corridor.
PATSU . . . . . . . Patrol Aircraft Service Unit.
Patwing . . . . . . . Patrol Wing
port . . . . . . . . . Left side, looking forward on ship or plane.
patrol . . . . . . . . *See:* mission.
picket ships . . . . . Usually destroyers; ships assigned to act as early warning radar screens.
PLE . . . . . . . . . Prudent Limit of Endurance. Point in flight when fuel supply dictates turning for home.
PPC . . . . . . . . . Patrol Plane Commander.

R&R . . . . . . . . Rest and recreation leave.
rpm . . . . . . . . . Revolutions per minute.

sack . . . . . . . . . Bed.
scuttlebutt . . . . . . Water fountain. Also, rumors, gossip.

Ships:
- American Navy:
  - AO . . . . . . Fleet oiler (tanker)
  - AV . . . . . . Seaplane tender
  - AV-10 . . . . Seaplane Tender No. 10: the USS *Chandeleur*.
  - AVP . . . . . Small seaplane tender
  - AVP-22 . . . . Seaplane Tender No. 22: the USS *Casco*.
  - CA . . . . . . Heavy cruiser
  - CL . . . . . . Light cruiser
  - CV . . . . . . Aircraft carrier
  - CVE . . . . . Escort aircraft carrier
  - CVL . . . . . Light aircraft carrier
  - DD . . . . . . Destroyer
  - DE . . . . . . Destroyer escort

| | | |
|---|---|---|
| LCI | . . . . . . | Landing craft, infantry |
| PC | . . . . . . . | Subchaser |
| PT | . . . . . . | Motor torpedo boat |

Japanese ships:
(Warships had same designations as U.S. ships)

| | | |
|---|---|---|
| Agano | . . . . . | Japanese cruiser (warship class). |
| Terutsuki | . . . . | Japanese destroyer (warship class). |

Commercial ships:

| | | |
|---|---|---|
| Fox Tare Able | . . | Freighter transport, 15,000 tons or more |
| Fox Tare Baker | . | Freighter transport, 8,000 or more tons |
| Fox Tare Charley | | Freighter transport, 3,000 to 8,000 tons |
| Fox Tare Dog | . . | Freighter transport, Up to 3,000 tons |
| Fox Uncle | . . . | A code name for a ship. |
| Lugger | . . . . . | Small barge type ship |
| Oiler | . . . . . . | Tanker |
| Sugar Charley Love | | A code name for a ship. |
| Sugar Dog | . . . | Freighter transport, small tonnage |
| Victor Able | . . . | A code name for a ship. |

Submarines:

| | | |
|---|---|---|
| I-5 | . . . . . . . | A class of ship (I) with the specific ship's designated number. |
| I-36 | . . . . . . | A class of ship (I) with the specific ship's designated number. |
| I-48 | . . . . . . | A class of ship (I) with the specific ship's designated number. |

| | | |
|---|---|---|
| ship's company | . . . . | Crew members of a ship. |
| ship's service | . . . . . | Navy "general store." |
| shit on a shingle | . . . | Nickname given to creamed, chipped beef or ground beef in a sauce, served on toast. Abbreviated by crews as: SOS. |
| small stores | . . . . . | Navy apparel store. |
| SOS | . . . . . . . . | The letters represented by the radio telegraphic signal (· · · – – – · · ·) used, especially by ships in distress, as an internationally recognized call for help; any call for help. *Also see:* shit on a shingle. |
| Spam | . . . . . . . . | The best-known menu item and the most despised—canned, compressed pieces of pork. |
| splashed | . . . . . . . | Shot down. |

| | |
|---|---|
| starboard | Right side, looking forward on ship or plane. |
| submarine safe zones | Sanctuary for U.S. submarines. |
| task force | A specific fleet of various types of ships. |
| tender | An auxiliary ship employed to attend one or more other ships or aircraft squadrons, supplying maintenance, provisions, etc. |
| TTSA | Transitional Training Squadron Atlantic. |
| Very light | A pyrotechnic signal in a system of signaling using white or colored balls of fire projected from a special pistol. Used especially to signal rescue planes or ships, by a crew in trouble. |
| Very pistol | A pistol for firing Very lights. |
| VH squadron | An air-sea rescue squadron. Also called a Dumbo squadron. |
| VP squadron | A Navy land- or sea-based air patrol squadron, using various aircraft like the PBM Mariner or the PB4Y Liberator. The *V* is a Navy designation meaning that the plane used is heavier than air; the *P* that it functions on patrol. |
| VPB squadron | Same as VP squadron. The designator was changed later in the war to include a *B*, which refers to the function of bombing as well as patrolling. |
| WAVES | Women Accepted for Volunteer Emergency Service: Women's Reserve of the U.S. Naval Reserve, the distinct force of women enlistees in the U.S. Navy, organized during World War II. |
| wingman | A plane that flies off your wing to support whatever activity you are involved in. |

*VPB-27's E-2 flying over the Golden Gate on a foggy morning. Everyone's favorite city! (Dick Gingrich photo collection)*

# SOURCES CITED

The following sources were used in this book:

Bureau of Aeronautics. Department of the Navy. 1944. *Pilot's Handbook of Flight Operating Instructions for the PBM-5 Mariner.* August.

Capt. Richard C. Knott, USN. 1979. *The American Flying Boat.* Annapolis, MD: Naval Institute Press.

Associated Press release. 1945. Courtesy of the Washington, D.C. *Times-Herald*.

Atkinson, Charles. 1944. *The Art of Buoy Making.* (Atkinson was PPC of Crew 3 of VPB-21.)

Hynes, Samuel. 1988. *Flights of Passage.* New York: Pocket Books (p. 104).

Mariner/Marlin Association and others. 1993. *Mariner/Marlin Anywhere, Anytime.* Paducah, KY: Turner Publishing Co. Used with permission of the publisher.

*Must We Repeat History?* 1997. Annapolis, MD: Naval Institute Proceedings. November.

Newsletters of the Mariner/Marlin Association. Used with blanket permission.

O'Neill, Richard. 1981. *Suicide Squads.* New York: Ballantine Books.

Owen, Charles A., ed. 1994. *USS Chandeleur AV-10: Sailing Airbase for Flying Boats.* Paducah, KY: Turner Publishing Co. Used with permission of the publisher.

Smith, Bob. 1990. "Patrolling the Pacific in the PBM Mariner." *Wings* August.

Sugrue, James (VPB-26). 1991. "The Mariner's Song," Mariner/Marlin Newsletter.

Sweet, Don. 1998. *The Sailor Aviators.* Ridgewood, NJ: Donald Sweet (originally published 1996 by Celo Valley Books, Burnsville, NC).

Y'Blood, William T. 1981. Red Sun Setting. Annapolis, MD: Naval Institute Press.

*The author today. (Don Sweet photo collection)*

*The author in 1945. (Don Sweet photo collection)*

# ABOUT THE AUTHOR

Donald Sweet volunteered for the U.S. Navy at seventeen. He attended aviation machinist mate and gunner and radar schools at Jacksonville, Florida, then served as a combat aircrewman in the Pacific theater of operations, flying some fifty missions. Returning home in mid-1945, he was assigned to train new crews. After discharge from the Navy in 1946 he attended Gettysburg College and graduated in 1949. He then worked for the U.S. Navy Department on Advanced Underseas Weapons Systems in various locations in the United States, and also in the Far East during the Korean War. The next twenty-five years were spent in the "corporate world," followed by ten years as a management consultant. He retired in 1991.

In 1972 he served on the Navy's Palenchar Task Force, which was instrumental in the development and initiation of the all-volunteer Navy.

Author of six business books, *The Sailor Aviators* was his first "story" book, and *Seaplanes at War* is number two. He resides in New Jersey with his wife, Joyce, near to his eight grandchildren.